THE SCHOOL REPORT

Nick Davies writes investigative stories for the *Guardian*, and in the last three years he has been named Journalist of the Year, Reporter of the Year and Feature Writer of the Year in British press awards. Apart from his work on newspapers, he also makes television documentaries and he has written three books: *White Lies*, which uncovered a racist miscarriage of justice in Texas; *Murder on Ward Four*, which examined the collapse of the NHS through the murder of children by Nurse Beverly Allitt; and *Dark Heart*, a journey through the wasteland of British poverty. He has three children and lives in Sussex.

WITHDRAWN
FROM
UNIVERSITIES
AT
MEDWAY
LIBRARY

ALSO BY NICK DAVIES

White Lies
Murder on Ward Four
Dark Heart

4581332

Nick Davies

THE SCHOOL REPORT

Why Britain's Schools are Failing

UNIVERSITIES AT MEDWAY LIBRARY

370.
941
DAV

VINTAGE

Published by Vintage 2000

2 4 6 8 10 9 7 5 3 1

Copyright © Nick Davies, 2000

The right of Nick Davies to be identified as the
author of this work has been asserted by him in accordance
with the Copyright, Designs and Patents Act, 1988

This book is sold subject to the condition that it shall
not, by way of trade or otherwise, be lent, resold, hired
out, or otherwise circulated without the publisher's
prior consent in any form of binding or cover other than
that in which it is published and without a similar condition including this condition being imposed on the
subsequent purchaser

All the pieces were originally published in the *Guardian*

First published in Great Britain in 2000 by
Vintage

Vintage
Random House, 20 Vauxhall Bridge Road,
London SW1V 2SA

Random House Australia (Pty) Limited
20 Alfred Street, Milsons Point, Sydney,
New South Wales 2061, Australia

Random House New Zealand Limited
18 Poland Road, Glenfield,
Auckland 10, New Zealand

Random House (Pty) Limited
Endulini, 5A Jubilee Road, Parktown 2193, South Africa

The Random House Group Limited Reg. No. 954009

www.randomhouse.co.uk

A CIP catalogue record for this book
is available from the British Library

ISBN 0 09 942216 6

A VINTAGE ORIGINAL

Papers used by Random House are natural,
recyclable products made from wood grown in sustainable forests;
the manufacturing processes conform to the environmental
regulations of the country of origin

Set in 10½/12 Sabon by SX Composing DTP, Rayleigh, Essex
Printed and bound in Great Britain by
Bookmarque Ltd, Croydon, Surrey

CONTENTS

THREE: PROBLEMS AND SOLUTIONS

FOREWORD

NOTHING I HAVE ever written has produced a reaction like the *Guardian* stories which are collected in this book – a torrent of readers' letters spilling over with passion, more than a hundred invitations to speak at public meetings, a couple of journalism awards and a personal denunciation from the Prime Minister and the Secretary of State for Education. The current *Guardian* editor says the response was of a different order to anything else he has seen since he took over the paper (and this is the editor who presided over the demise of Aitken, Hamilton and Mandelson). What was that about?

I think something rather odd happened. Normally, when you publish an investigation in a newspaper, you hope you are uncovering something which nobody knows. With these stories, however, we did the reverse – we delivered something which masses of people knew but which no one with any power would admit. That torrential response was not shock or horror but a clamour of recognition of a reality that was being denied. And there's the real lesson of *The School Report*.

In the eighteen months I spent researching these stories, I got deeper into the workings of a government department than I have ever done before. It was not a reassuring experience. I went into this with a vague feeling of unspecified benevolence towards the Secretary of State for Education, David Blunkett, largely because he carried the torch in Sheffield local government during the dark days of the 1980s. I came out with a feeling close to contempt, having peered into a department which, I eventually concluded, was habitually lying and cheating and was presiding over a shambles – something it was enabled to do mainly by the scale of that selfsame dishonesty.

I came away with a picture of ministers beset by problems and lost for solutions – lost, either because they simply didn't understand the issues well enough to know what to do, or because they did know and couldn't bear the political consequences. Rather than admit they were stuck, they were reaching for pseudo-solutions, policies which gave them something to talk about, offered the appearance of action, threw the pundits something to chew on while the real problems lay unsolved in the background, because (as the ministers often very well knew) the alleged solutions were entirely bogus, bound to fail.

Look at the story of Fresh Start, David Blunkett's brave new cure for the weakest schools – and at the weight of evidence which had discredited the idea in the United States, where it originated in 1984, long before Mr Blunkett ever pulled it out of his briefcase and started to wave it around like a magic wand. Look at 'special measures', the routine procedure for dealing with a school that has failed its Ofsted report: pause for a moment over the statistic we dug up (after months of negotiation to get access to them) and compare them to the ministers' grandiose claims of success. Or look at the official claims for the virtues of the DFEE's 'mentoring' scheme, set against the department's own devastating findings of its miserable weakness. This is high-octane guff. The underlying problem, as you will see in the first two or three stories, is that the entire strategy of Mr Blunkett's department is based on an analysis of school failure which has the intellectual weight of a joke in a Christmas cracker. Everything else flows from that analysis, and the simple reality is that it's phoney.

And then there are the outright lies. These collected stories are slightly different from the original versions which ran in the *Guardian* – slightly longer, because we have not had to cut them for space, edited for book publication and slightly amended to avoid the repetition of themes which is necessary when you are spreading out information in stories published over a period of twelve months. But the content is the same. So you will see, in one of the early stories, how we gave credit to David Blunkett for securing a £19 billion increase in funding for education – and then you'll see how, a few months later, we discovered that we had been conned. Well, how the whole country had been conned. Here is a Secretary of State who takes the central core of his departmental activity – his budget, the fuel for every move he makes – presents it to Parliament, press and public, and grossly and repeatedly lies about it. And he gets away with it. To be precise, he was taken to task only once, in the House of Commons, by the Liberal Democrat education spokesman, Phil Willis. Hansard records the Secretary of State's reaction. He laughed. And that was that (although he never again repeated the £19 billion lie).

This is a lesson not just about the cynicism of politicians but also about our own gullibility – particularly our gullibility as journalists. We allow Whitelaw to manage us: Mr Blunkett makes a big announcement about extra funds for Fresh Start schools; we report it, as though there were some kind of sense in it; and then we go off into micro-criticism of its detail – whether this is quite enough extra cash, whether there is really such a thing as a superhead – without explaining that the whole project is a proven failure. We are pushed into a sideshow.

Within a week of Mr Blunkett first telling his £19 billion whopper, he was caught out by the Treasury Select Committee, who exposed the most successful of his several sleights of hand. They did the same for the then Health Secretary, Frank Dobson, whose claims about new cash for his department were similarly fictitious. The point is that the press missed the story. The Treasury Select Committee's report sank like a stone, the journalists chased off to the next press conference, and the various ministers carried on fibbing for eighteen months before they were caught out. (Frank Dobson's budget was exposed as a hoax by BBC *Panorama*, by coincidence, in the week after we took apart Mr Blunkett's.)

I spent the first three or four months of this research being as stupid as it is possible for a journalist to be without getting sacked. I started, in the approved fashion, by reading files of old newspaper stories; I read the book by the former education minister, George Walden; I went to see senior people at the Department for Education and Ofsted. And I emerged with the clear view that school failure was primarily caused by bad teachers, and in particular by bad teachers who had been led astray by 'trendy teaching methods' from the 1960s. Then two things happened. First, I read a book called *Failing School Failing City* by Martin Johnson, a veteran teacher and now president of the NAS/UWT union. Then I started going into schools. And I realised that my working theory was complete garbage, that the truth was simpler, nastier and very plain to see, as the first two stories, set in Sheffield, should make clear: you cannot make sense of why some schools fail and some succeed without taking account of the corrosive impact of child poverty, which has soared in this country in the last twenty years. Combine that with the effects of the Conservative education reforms of the late 1980s and you have a design for educational failure.

You can look at any area of our schooling system – the effect of private schools on their state counterparts, the scale and distribution of funding, teacher stress and teacher pay, syllabus and teaching technique, truancy and exclusion, the outbreak of teacher cheating in exams – and you will not be able to make sense of it unless you take primary account of child poverty and Kenneth Baker's reforms. There are other factors in there as well, but those two are essential. And yet David Blunkett has sidelined them and laid down a smoke-screen of pseudo-solutions.

My earlier willingness to swallow completely the easy official line, that failure was simply the result of poor teaching, reflected not so much ignorance as a kind of lazy-minded stupidity. I had spent the previous four years writing a book called *Dark Heart*, all about poverty in Britain and the damage it was inflicting on people, particularly children. I knew more about this than most people, and yet I had completely failed to make the connection. I had ended up in the sideshow – because that was where everyone else was.

Mr Blunkett has chosen to remain there. The reality is that unless he acknowledges the fundamental effect of child poverty and unless he finds the political courage to scrap almost all of the market-driven reforms of the late 1980s, none of the dinky little schemes which he has launched will save our schools from crisis.

Speaking of courage, there are several people whose help on these stories was outstanding. Jan Woodhead, then the head teacher of Abbeydale Grange School in Sheffield, knew it was risky to allow a reporter to run around her school without any kind of restraint. She knew, too, that someone somewhere had to let the light in on the truth, so she took the risk. Her staff supported her. Afterwards – predictably – she caught it in the neck from several of Mr Blunkett's loyalists. She stood up to that, too, and has since been promoted to a new job running one of the biggest schools in the country. I would like to register my gratitude and respect for her and her staff. They are great people.

A lot of other people put themselves out on my behalf: Camila Batmanghelidjh of Kids Company; Dr Phil Budgell, the former chief inspector of Sheffield's schools; Tim Brighouse, the director of education in Birmingham; Libby Coleman, the former head teacher of Marina High School in Brighton; Dick Davison of the Independent Schools Information Service; Barry Dawson of the National Primary Heads Association; Nigel de Gruchy of the NAS/UWT; Peter Lampl of the Sutton Trust; Margaret Maden of the Centre for Successful Schools; Patricia Metham, the head teacher of Roedean College; Dr J.J. Molenaar, head teacher at Martinus College in Grootebroek, northern Holland; Professor Peter Mortimore of the Institute of Education; Mary O'Hagan, who works for the Lib Dems in the House of Commons; Alan Parker, the director of education for Ealing; Lord Puttnam; Nigel Sagar of the Barking and Dagenham LEA; Edna Speed of Save the Family; Simon Szreter of St John's College in Cambridge; Henk Verreijen, head teacher of Tabor School in Hoorn in Holland; Gale Waller of the Local Government Association; Dr Anne West of the London School of

Economics; Sir David Winkley, the former head of Grove Primary School in Birmingham; Chris Woodhead of Ofsted; Michaela Wouters of Nottingham University, as well as rather a lot of Ofsted inspectors whose wisdom and understanding is sadly lost behind the headline-grabbing of their controversial chief inspector.

The editor of the *Guardian*, Alan Rusbridger, allowed me vast amounts of time to research and space to write. These are rare things in Fleet Street today; without him, none of this would have happened. Finally, I would like to thank my research assistant, Helene Mulholland, who made an enormous contribution to every one of these stories.

ONE

THE TRUTH ABOUT FAILING SCHOOLS

POVERTY INVADES THE CLASSROOM

14 SEPTEMBER 1999

THIS IS THE moment. The teacher with the bleeper has legs like an ostrich and takes the stairs three at a time. Within thirty seconds he has reached the classroom which has called for help, and there he wades into the confusion. The trouble is Terence.

Terence is on a computer but he is refusing to work on the exercise he has been set. Instead he is fooling with graphics, simply ignoring instructions, his chin resting insolently on one palm. The classroom teacher is torn between Terence, who is stealing his attention, and the other children, who are beginning to wander and chatter. The teacher on Bleeper Patrol tells Terence he must leave the room. Terence sullenly refuses and carries on toying with the screen in front of him. Two girls come over to eavesdrop on the confrontation. In the background, several boys break into Punjabi to swap insults.

This is the moment that lies at the heart of the often frantic debate about Britain's schools – when a teacher stands up in front of a class and the teaching simply fails to take place. It is the moment which haunts a prime minister who famously declared that his three highest priorities are 'education, education and education'. And this particular moment happens to be occurring in a school which sits right in the centre of Sheffield, the political cradle of the current education secretary, David Blunkett.

The Bleeper Man persists. He has been on this kind of patrol many times before, acting as a kind of fireman who can be called out to deal with any crisis in the building. Tantrums, fights, breaking windows, smoking cigarettes, all riddled in amongst the daily rituals of a stable school. On a bad day, the bleeper will call for help forty or fifty times – a crisis every eight minutes or so. He knows he has to be careful. A few weeks ago, a boy went up on the roof and dangled one leg over the edge, threatening to jump unless he was left alone. That time, the Bleeper Man quietly talked him down.

For several minutes, with the whole class wobbling on the verge of disintegration, Terence simply ignores the requests to leave, until suddenly he jumps to his feet, crashes his way through several unused chairs, sneers at the classroom teacher and surges out into the corridor, where he marches off, drumming one fist loudly against the wall. In the doorway at the end, he bumps into a twelve-year-old girl, kicks her in the shin and vanishes around the corner. The class calms down, the teacher teaches and the Bleeper Man goes off in search of Terence, the electronic alarm already squealing once more in his pocket.

Abbeydale Grange* was once the cream of Sheffield's schools, a well-endowed comprehensive which was built out of three grammar schools – two for girls and one for boys – with a tradition of high achievement and old-fashioned discipline. In many ways it still succeeds, and yet now it is beset by trouble. It struggles to survive; its numbers have slumped, from more than 2,000 to just over 500; only 22% of the pupils score five A to C grades at GCSE; its budget is drowning in deficit. It is one of the 40% of secondary schools in Britain which are said by the Office of State Education (Ofsted) to fall below the required standard.

Why do some schools fail to deliver the best academic results? The big problem is trendy teaching methods (according to just about everybody on the right); it's a chronic shortage of resources (just about everybody on the left); it's teachers (Ofsted); it's Ofsted (teachers); it's a culture of low expectation (George Walden, the former Tory education minister); it's an overdose of intervention (the teacher

---

* To protect the privacy of children at Abbeydale Grange, most of their names and some minor identifying details have been changed.

unions); it's the abolition of grammar schools; the existence of private schools; the rigging of exam results; the shortage of nursery schools. It's the most important question in British public life. And yet the answer is torn like a fox between hounds.

This matters not simply as an exercise in failed analysis – there are plenty of policy questions which remain unanswered – but because in the last fifteen years education has attracted more intervention than any other area of government. From the sweeping Tory reforms of the late 1980s to the volley of initiatives since May 1997, this cacophony of answers has generated a cross-fire of activity by the state. If the analysis is wrong, much of this activity has been volleys shot into the dark.

Why do schools fail? Despite all the confusion, there is an answer to the question. The strange reality is that in an area which is so peculiarly riven with controversy and genuine doubt, there is one clear, undeniable truth – one factor which more than any other determines whether a school will succeed or fail in delivering academic results. It is something which is recognised by almost everyone who is directly involved in schools, and yet it remains overlooked by almost all outsiders and sidelined by almost all official discourse. The answer is revealed by the Bleeper Man.

It is ten o'clock in the morning at Abbeydale Grange, and already the bleeper has been busy: Dave has casually walked out of his class and gone to see his mates two doors away; a Somali lad with a baseball cap has downed tools and will not work; Joey is dancing on a table, whistling loudly so he cannot hear his teacher's protests. The Bleeper Man ricochets between them, ferrying the unruly to the Time Out room, where he finds Darren, who is not supposed to be there at all. He was excluded yesterday, but his mother has sent him to school just the same. It is a contest with disorder.

Here on the wall is Shane's poem, one eleven-year-old boy's image of education:

School's crap, school's good
Every day, we come to school
It always rains
And every day I get off my bus and go for a fag
I say to myself 'Well, there goes another day'
Teachers talking, students shouting
When is all this noise going to stop?

Here comes Imran, long and lean and full of mouth, sauntering late into class with a bag of crisps on the go, stopping to chat to his friends on the way to his desk. Never mind the lesson struggling to survive. Never mind anything. Imran is already on a last warning. He threatened to take off his belt and thrash someone who crossed him and the head teacher has told him he is on the edge of the precipice staring down at permanent exclusion. He has promised to produce 'a ten-out-of-ten' day. Now, he grins as he swaggers towards his seat, a little lord of disorder.

What is going on in this place? It is not that the school is in chaos. There are no riots or rapes. Indeed, there are classrooms full of children who are learning. There are charismatic teachers and some brilliant kids – charming, clever kids, sporting stars, girls taking their GCSEs two and three years ahead of schedule. But then there is this fragility, this constant bubbling of trouble threatening to erupt as if the teachers were pulling off a miracle every time they reached the end of a lesson without an explosion. As the Bleeper Man lopes through the school, juggling crises, the outline of the truth begins to emerge, slowly through the blizzard of contradictory claims.

He talks about the day he followed an eleven-year-old boy who had skived off class. When he caught up with him, he asked him simply 'What's up?', and the boy slumped on to his stomach on the floor and started beating the lino with his fists, groaning with some inexpressible pain. He talks about the boy with the elfin face, who is sent to the Time Out room three times today: he has no father, his mother cannot cope; he has an alarming medical problem and he knows it; he is eleven but he has the reading age of a six-year-old; his dearest wish is to be excluded permanently so that he does not have to deal with life in the classroom.

There is the boy who comes to school from some kind of hell with his mother and spends the day hiding in the hood of his coat; the girl who has lost her mother and her father and whose grandparents were so harsh with her that she went to social services and begged to be taken into care; the boy whose home burned down, killing his pet while he fought with the firemen who would not let him go into the flames to save it (and who is now obsessed with doom and destruction). There are girls who get pregnant, boys who get drug problems, kids who have been taught at home to beat the crap out of anyone who irritates them, a boy who has moved home seven times in seven months because neighbours keep attacking his mother – and several times a week, he disappears from school and trails back to their latest refuge to protect her.

There are twelve-year-old girls who are the main carers in their family, feeding, clothing and supervising a cluster of younger siblings. This girl's brother has been beaten up by the local street gang. This boy's father is in prison. Somebody's mother is a drunk. Somebody's house has been torched by the neighbours. Here's an art class of thirteen-year-olds who have just spent the day in Derbyshire: half of them had never left Sheffield city in their lives. Here's a girl who has gone to the school office because her leg hurts, only to find that the police want to talk to her about reports that her stepfather has been assaulting her.

The children who are caught up by the Bleeper Patrol have more stories than Hollywood, but almost all of them have one thing in common. They are poor. And that is what matters. It is a simple thing. Every teacher knows it. There was a time when every government minister admitted it. The banal reality is that the single factor which more than any other determines a school's performance is its intake – the children who go there.

A small part of this is gender: girls at secondary school do better than boys. Everybody puzzles over it, but nobody can deny it. No single-sex girls' school, for example, has ever been failed by Ofsted. While 40% of Sheffield girls scored at least five A to C grades at GCSE last year, only 33% of boys did so. But the big factor is poverty.

7

If a school takes in a substantial proportion of children who come from a disadvantaged background – if their parents do not read, if they have no books at home, if they are awake half the night and then half asleep all day, if they have been emotionally damaged by problems in their family or in their community, if they have suffered from an environment which, more than any other, is likely to expose them to drug abuse and violence and alcohol abuse and the collapse of social boundaries – then the school is more likely to fail academically. A school which is based in a disadvantaged community will struggle with its children; one that is based in a more affluent area will prosper.

This is not an occasional problem, but an endemic one. There are about 13.3 million children in Britain. On any available measure, some 4.6 million live in poverty – and they are all enrolled in schools. The evidence that poverty undermines education is overwhelming – and has been for decades. Yet governments deny it. The last government denied the poverty itself. This government admits the poverty but denies its impact.

By obscuring this simple reality, the public discourse on our school system has entered the realm of the absurd and become lost there. This is not to deny that there are good and bad teachers, that there are good and bad approaches to teaching, that schools can make a difference. It is not to quarrel with the complaint that schools in the 1960s and 70s were allowed to drift into a state of unsupervised complacency, or that ideologies of social engineering may often have interfered with education, or that the *Guardian* among others on the left was seduced into some naive and unsupportable positions. But when those factors take their proper place in the picture, they slip out to the margins while the children hold the centre – and the host of political initiatives which ignore the children are revealed as mere alibis. Like all alibis, those initiatives may contain some element of truth, but like all of the most dangerous alibis, they are essentially dishonest.

Until a few years ago, Dr Phil Budgell was the chief inspector of schools in Sheffield. Like his opposite number in every other local education Authority (LEA), he visited all the schools on his patch and noted their strengths and shortcomings, but unlike most of his opposite numbers Dr Budgell is a trained statistician. In search of an understanding of what he saw, he began to sift through the river of statistics which flowed into his department, panhandling it in search of patterns.

The poverty was obvious. Since 1979, South Yorkshire has lost 24% of its jobs, and nearly a quarter of Sheffield's children now live in families with no earner. Dr Budgell started using census material to tot up the indicators of poverty in each household – no earner, no car, overcrowding, single parent, ethnic minority. Then he switched to the database for the city's schools, pulled out the postcodes for every single pupil, matched this against the districts for which he had census data and produced an index of disadvantage for all the schools in Sheffield. He factored in the distribution of girl pupils and also figures for those who simply failed to turn up for school in Year Eleven, when exams were being taken, and he produced a table which ranked all twenty-seven secondary schools in the city according to the difficulties of their intake.

Then he looked at the academic outcomes of the twenty-seven schools. He used seven different measures of exam results, including average scores, mean scores, A to C grades, A to G grades. There were small variations but essentially the picture was clear: the league table of schools who did well in exams was simply the reverse of the league table of difficult intakes. Using multiple regression analysis, Dr Budgell found that more than 90% of the difference in exam results between schools was accounted for simply by the poverty, gender and final-year attendance of the children who were enrolled there. What was being done by the schools was influencing only the remaining 5 to 10%.

'I'm not saying that schools don't make a difference,' he told the *Guardian*. 'There are incompetent teachers, but in order to explain the failing of inner-city schools in terms of incompetence you have to make the bizarre assumption that these schools have hired a mass of incompetent teachers while good schools have hired none. There is a volume of evidence that schools are not playing on a level playing field. When you look at these intake factors, the level playing field is more like the side of Mount Everest.'

Three secondary schools in Sheffield have been condemned by Ofsted and put into 'special measures': Earl Marshall, Hinde House and Myrtle Springs. All three are in the northeast of the city, with an intake which is dominated by the children of poor families. At Fir Vale School, which has taken over from Earl Marshall, the head teacher, Ken Cook, has a pupil body of whom only 16% speak English as their first language. Most of his parents speak no English at all. On a Monday morning last term, he had seven Somali children turn up for their first day at school, fresh out of a war zone, without a sentence of English between them. 'Within an hour they are in the classroom,' he said, 'and we are accountable for their performance.'

At Hinde House School, the head teacher, Sarah Draper, deals with a similarly poor intake: 'If there are twenty-five kids in a classroom, there may be fifteen with behavioural problems. I am past being shocked, although I know that people out there don't understand.' One person who is close to the school recalled the children who had cut their classes during England's first match in the World Cup last year. Some of their parents had insisted that the children were right to stay at home. 'They thought football was more important than school. The trouble is that education is a middle-class value which we are trying to operate in a working-class culture.'

Abbeydale Grange draws its children from a wedge of deprivation that takes in the Sharrow area where unemployment is the highest in the city, infant mortality is the highest in the city, 30% of children come from families on income support, 12% of the adults are diagnosed as suffering from depression and 25% of the children live in homes officially deemed to be overcrowded. Fifty-three per cent of the school's students claim free school meals – the most commonly used measure of poverty in schools: on national trends, a further 10% would be poor enough to qualify but fail to lodge the claim. The poverty invades the school like water flooding a ship, reaching into every weak point.

Poverty, at first, means sheer material hardship: the numerous children who come to school without breakfast; the boy who falls down in the mud at school and turns up for the rest of the week in the same muddy clothes; the homes which have no books, never mind computers or Internet connections; no quiet place for homework; no cash for school trips; no cash for bus fares in the morning.

Poverty often means parents who gained nothing from school and expect nothing more from it for their children, like the Somali father who keeps his daughter at home so that she can translate for him; or the man who has kept his thirteen-year-old boy off school for the last two years so he can help look after their animals. Abbeydale teachers last term told Wayne, who is twelve, that he should start to think about what GCSEs he wants to sit. He blinked and shook his head and said that no one in his family – none of his numerous older brothers and sisters, and certainly not his parents or their siblings – had ever passed any exam of any kind, so, well, why would he?

Head teachers and officials at the town hall agree that in the old public housing estates, education has never been highly valued. In the good old days up until the early 1980s, that was because there were apprenticeships more or less on demand in the coal and steel industries. Now, Sheffield's traditional economy has been destroyed, 60% of the old industrial jobs have been lost for ever, and the reasoning is reversed: last year, one out of every five young people who left Sheffield's schools had no work to go to, and one out of nine had no qualifications at all. Overwhelmingly, those young people came from the old estates where they remain now, as the neighbours – and role models – of this year's students.

The best available source of income and status is the drugs economy, which reaches into every school in the city. One of the Abbeydale Grange teachers recalls the primary school he taught at where one of the eight-year-old boys daily stole the lunchboxes from other kids: he was the son of the local drug baron, so no one could argue with him. In the library at Abbeydale, Mark, now aged fifteen, tells how the previous day he bumped into a friend from primary school. 'I never knew him that well. He wasn't exactly a friend. But he gave me his bleeper number in case I wanted to buy any blow off him. Which was helpful.' Why bother with school?

Poverty steers children off course long before they reach secondary school. Of the 115 eleven-year-olds in last term's Year Seven at Abbeydale Grange, twenty-five arrived at the school with a reading age of less than eight. Their Non-Verbal Reasoning Scores were just as low. The effect on the rest of their school is catastrophic.

Many of the deprived children come from families of recent immigrants who do not speak English as their first language. Of the 521 pupils in the school last term, 204 are from the Indian subcontinent, together with children from Colombia, Brazil, Somalia, Venezuela, Kosovo, Senegal, Portugal and China. Half of the pupils in Years Seven and Eight are in the process of learning English. In Years Eight and Nine, the position is even more difficult, with 70% of students adapting to English as a second language. Last term, one boy completed a French test by translating the text into Albanian. By the end of the term, the teacher had found someone to make sense of it and discovered that he had got almost all of it right.

Poverty does its worst damage with the emotions of those who live with it: parents who are too tired or depressed, too stretched trying to juggle too many young children, too damaged to cope; children whose development is distorted from their earliest days. Forty-five per cent of the students at Abbeydale Grange are classified as having special educational needs, many suffer from emotional or behavioural problems. Twelve per cent of them have a need so serious that they are 'statemented' by the local authority as cases requiring the involvement of outside agencies: IQ as low as 50, very short concentration, hyperactivity, disruptive behaviour, attention-seeking, dyslexia, clinical depression.

Josh suffers from a classic cluster of problems. He is twelve, his father has not been seen for years, his stepfather can't be bothered with him, his mother drinks and simply does not like him. She criticises his every move and has called the school to complain about their sending home letters in praise of his better behaviour. When a teacher tried to take him to the cinema as a reward for trying, she blocked it. Josh expects to make a mess of everything he touches and he spends the day in school avoiding work for fear of failing; looking for attention with disruptive jokes and antics; smoking and attempting to wander off to the shops. There are children like Josh in every class in Abbeydale Grange.

So a school like this is logged as a failure, its academic results limping far behind the private schools and the state schools in rural towns and pleasant suburbs. Back on the Bleeper Patrol, however, a very different picture begins to emerge – signs of success, hidden beneath the surface of daily school life.

During the night it rained, and as usual the puddles on the flat school roof have leaked through to the modern languages room below. Now there's a whole Spanish class roaming the corridors in search of a home. The Bleeper Man races down the corridor, finds an empty room and races back to the Spanish class, but before he can reach them he finds a small girl wandering in search of a teacher who has failed to show up. He sends the girl to tell the Spanish class to go to the empty room, pops his head in the door of the class without a teacher and calms the children, gallops off down the stairs to the staff room, finds the name of the missing teacher on the rota, heads to the school office, who have no idea where he is, charges back upstairs, shepherding stray Spanish students as he goes, tells two boys to stop spitting and a third not to swear, grabs some litter off the floor, finds a spare teacher, sends him to the class who have lost theirs, checks that the Spanish class has found its home and sees that all is well, heads for the class without a teacher and sees they are still fooling around, discovers the spare teacher has gone to the wrong classroom, finds him, redirects him, takes a breath . . . and realises that all is well, all is quiet. He has created order.

While the outside world looks at the league tables and sees failure, for the teachers inside the school, life is thick with success.

One of the Bleeper Man's most regular customers was

Catherine, who left the school this summer. She came from a violent and broken home and, from her first day in school, was an almost constant source of disruption, walking out of classes, refusing to fit in, threatening violence against herself and others. The school poured its attention into her. They attached a support assistant to her, designed a special timetable for her, allowed her to go to a Quiet Room to escape from her most worrying classes, drew up a contract for her behaviour, reviewed her progress every week, gave her counselling, liaised with her unstable home. And it worked. Last summer term, she sat her GCSE exams. After five years of domestic turmoil and emotional pain, the school had no illusions at all about the grades she would get. But she sat them – decided it was worth the effort, decided to revise, decided to turn up on time and even to sit through them writing, decided to try. That is success.

When the Bleeper Man sees Josh in the playground being approached by two older boys on their way for a cigarette, and Josh turns them away, that, too, is success. When Terence rushes out of his computer class and disappears and the Bleeper Man quietly follows him and finally discovers him already sitting in the Time Out room, having decided to cooperate and not to run or to fight, that is success.

These are children who are so tough on the streets that policemen won't go on their estates without back-up and flak jackets; yet a lone teacher in shirtsleeves deals with them thirty at a time. But that doesn't score points in the league tables. The same children who fail their SATs (Standard Assessment Tests) tests also write the school prospectus and sit on interview panels, with a power of veto, when the school hires new staff.

There is hidden success in sport – like the Abbeydale Grange football team which struggled to win matches but scored a city-wide record by playing for the five full years of a school career without ever arguing with a single referee's decision. They were rewarded by Sheffield United, who invited them to use their ground at Bramall Lane to play their final match. There is social success, in the tumultuous combination of cultures in the playground without any kind of race hatred; in the rarity of bullying; in the sheer delight of the Year Seven cricket team who have only tennis balls and four elderly bats for practice but who took on the local Birkdale prep school with their brand-new kit – and thrashed them.

When a Year Ten student passes GCSE maths a year early, when two Year Nine students do it two years early, when a Year Eight student does it three years early, that is straightforward academic success, although none of it shows up in the official school tables which record only Year Eleven results. When the government last year produced a 'value-added' table, concentrating not on exam results but on signs of academic improvement between Years Nine and Eleven, Abbeydale Grange was one of only three schools in the whole of Sheffield to record a dramatic improvement. But other schools, who normally come out top of the tables, complained – and the whole exercise was watered down.

The bell rings for the end of the last lesson. The Bleeper Man heads out to the driveway, where the children mill around the buses. The outside world is waiting to invade. Two young men with pimples and baseball caps start handing out advertising flyers for a free evening at a new nightclub in the city centre. The eleven-year-old boys and girls grab the flyers and mount the buses. Two girls from Year Seven hug each other tight and say goodbye for the day. A couple of boys slip away for a cigarette.

Schools are defined by the children who go there. Take the children from Abbeydale Grange and parachute them into Eton, and Eton will start to fail academically. Take Eton's teachers and plant them in Abbeydale Grange, and they will struggle to teach. The truth is masked by academic results. They simply disclose how well the children did in their exams, but they don't tell you how well the school did with its intake. And it is the intake that matters. For years, Britain has been shovelling children into poverty – taking away their parents' work, cutting their family's welfare, embroiling them in a war against drugs which has plunged them into crime and violence, breaking up their communities – and now these children are in the schools, screwed up, damaged and delinquent, shunted over the edge. A school with a poor intake is like an ambulance at the bottom of a cliff: sometimes it can pick up the children and patch up the damage; most of the time it's too late.

One of the teachers at Abbeydale Grange left at the end of last term, abandoning his career twenty years early. 'Opinion-formers seem to have no concept of what is going on,' he said. 'The general level of achievement of children with these problems is very low and it has got worse with poverty.' This particular teacher has found his own solution. He is a Christian and he has gone off to join the Church Army in the hope that God might succeed where governments have failed.

The point here is not that governments should introduce a more sensitive measure of achievement like value-added tables. The lesson goes much further: the vast majority of government interventions over the last fifteen years have been built on the foundation that schools can be blamed for the failure of their children; if that foundation is essentially false, the whole structure of reform is wrong. Millions of pounds and a mass of energy have been poured into projects which at best succeed only partially, and at worst actively damage the schools they are claiming to help.

Poverty and schools

This is the secret that everyone knows: the children of poor families are far less likely to do well in school than those whose parents are affluent. For the last ten years, this has been almost buried in denial. 'Poverty is no excuse,' according to the Department for Education. Nevertheless, it is the key. As everyone knows.

The ministers and pundits who want to deny or diminish the link are keen to present it as the invention of soft-focus lefties trying to justify a socialist theory of education or to excuse incompetent teachers. However, the clearest and most persuasive recent evidence for the link was produced earlier this year, not by a teacher's union or a liberal academic but by the Treasury, in its fourth report on the modernisation of Britain's tax and benefit system. Reviewing nearly thirty years of research, the Treasury reported:

'Children from disadvantaged backgrounds are much less likely to succeed in education... On 'difficult to let' estates, one in four children gain no GCSEs (the national average is one in twenty) and rates of truancy are four times the national average ... There is considerable evidence that growing up in a family which has experienced financial difficulties, damages children's educational performance...

The differences between advantaged and disadvantaged children are apparent from a very early age. At 22 months, children whose parents are in social classes one or two are already fourteen percentage points higher up in the educational-development distribution than children whose parents are in social class four or five ... The data from the National Child Development Survey show that there is a strong relationship between children's performance in maths and reading tests between the ages of six and eight, and their parents' earnings, with the children of higher-earning parents performing better . . . If one father's earnings are double the level of another, his son's maths test score is on average five percentile points higher than the other's ... Going to school does not reduce the differences in early development between advantaged and disadvantaged children.'

The link is strong. It is also central to the experience of Britain's schools because, as the same Treasury document confirms, poverty in Britain has trebled since 1979 to the point where a third of Britain's children – more than four million of them – now live below the poverty line. This torrent of poor children poured into the classroom at exactly the same time as standards of behaviour and achievement slumped. Our levels of pupil failure are higher than in most of the rest of the developed world, but our levels of child poverty are also higher than in most of the rest of the developed world. According to Eurostat, for example, 32% of children in the UK live in poor households, compared to 20% in the rest of the European Union. According to Treasury figures, we have higher poverty levels than Greece and Portugal.

The physical, emotional and social damage which is inflicted on children who live in poverty is clearly reflected in the latest academic results. The independent group, Research and Information on State Education, trawled through Ofsted reports and matched the standards of students against the number who were claiming free school meals, the nearest available measure of poverty in the classroom. In schools with only a few poor children, one in every five pupils was scoring Grade 1; at the other end of the spectrum, in schools with a well above average number of children on free school meals, only one in a hundred was doing so.

A disadvantaged intake can make life tough for a whole school, not just for individuals. Researchers at Durham University looked at schools which have been failed and subjected to 'special measures' by Ofsted and then matched them against the six bands of disadvantage which are used by the Department of Education to reflect the proportion of pupils on free meals. Not one of the schools in special measures fell into any of the three 'affluent' bands. A small group fell close to the national average, but almost all of them – 96.5% – were in the two upper bands, schools with a proportion of children on free meals which is clearly above the national average.

The evidence goes on and on – from the US, the OECD, the EU. There are literally dozens of academic studies which confirm the link between poverty and academic failures. But in the Department of Education, anxious to deliver policies which appear to promise short-term success, the new orthodoxy remains the same. 'Poverty is no excuse.'

How government has buried the truth

The greatest dream of all good experts is to find a government who will listen and turn their research into reality. Some succeed. Peter Mortimore did. But the greatest frustration for any expert is to have found a government who finally listened – and ended up misunderstanding.

In 1975, Peter Mortimore abandoned a nine-year career as a schoolteacher to join a team of researchers who were about to embark on a special project for Professor Michael Rutter at the Institute of Psychiatry at the University of London. The goal which Mortimore and his colleagues set themselves was to try to identify the seeds of success in the classroom by spending four years studying a dozen schools in London. They were to ignite one of the longest running theoretical disputes in the world of education. In 1979 they published Fifteen Thousand Hours: Secondary Schools and Their Effects on Children. It was a ground-breaking work. It challenged the conventional wisdom of the time by showing that although the social and economic background of pupils was a very powerful factor in deciding academic results, nevertheless it was not the whole story. Schools could make a difference, and they tried to identify the kinds of things which successful schools could do for their pupils to start to overcome their inherent social disadvantage.

This was important. There was no disguising the fact that state schools were in trouble. Numerous schools had been renamed 'comprehensive' without any training for staff or change in their curriculum. Local education authorities allowed their schools to be accountable to just about no one. Head teachers could be as secretive as they pleased, concealing their results and disguising their problems, failing to heed criticism or complaint. There was widespread concern that some teaching methods were sloppy and ineffective and that 'child-centred' learning had reached a point of absurdity where teachers declined to mark their students' work for fear of appearing critical. Many schools appeared to have low expectations of their students, reflected in indifferent results. Now, finally, there was a chance to spread the best practice, to make schools more effective.

It took nearly ten years for the message to get through to the Department of Education. By that time, the research had been confirmed and refined repeatedly, in the United States as well as in Britain, and there was real excitement about a cluster of possibilities for school improvement – some involving different approaches to leadership and management, some to classroom technique. But when they finally acted, Conservative ministers grabbed the wrong end of the *stick and started beating teachers over the back with it. They fired off a volley of reforms – league tables, SATs tests, Ofsted inspections – all of which were aimed at the kind of School Effectiveness that Mortimore and his colleagues had identified and all of which utterly ignored the fact that the social and economic background of pupils remained a very powerful factor.*

Mortimore and others tried to warn them. They explained that the most you could hope to achieve by improving schools was an increase of between 8 and 10% in results: it mattered, but it was only a fraction of the whole. It was like watching a furious motorist pumping up the tyres on a car which had run out of petrol: it might eventually help the car to run more smoothly, but while he refused to address the real problem it would do very little good, and sooner or later, if he just carried on pumping regardless, something was bound to blow.

By now, Mortimore had become one of the leading experts on education in the country and had been appointed head of the Institute of Education at the University of London. In a book called Road to Improvement *he warned: 'It is crucial that policy makers desist from claiming that school improvement – by itself and in the absence of extra resources – can solve all the problems. Whilst this might be true in "advantaged" schools, it is certainly not true in disadvantaged schools.' Rather like the atom scientists who saw their work hijacked by government for immoral ends, he saw his warnings ignored.*

The difficulty was that School Effectiveness was immensely attractive to politicians. By pinpointing the work of teachers and administrators, it completely absolved central government of all possible responsibility for failure. By sidelining the impact of intake, it permitted policies which focused on detail in the school and were therefore relatively cheap, and which promised to deliver quick results and were therefore electorally attractive. And so the Department for Education and Ofsted were already committed to hunting down failing schools and attributing their failure entirely to the weakness of teachers and managers, ignoring the destructive impact of

20

an intake which had become progressively more delinquent as the new poverty swept through the country. The government's supporters were determined to recognise part of the truth and nothing but that part of the truth. Conservative columnists savaged Mortimore's book, effectively accusing him of not understanding his own research.

Ofsted and education ministers justified themselves by pointing to the performance of a group of schools with a disadvantaged intake, who appeared to have succeeded against the odds. The National Commission on Education organised studies of eleven such schools and found there was real evidence that, despite their intake, these schools had succeeded, using a combination of strong leadership, the setting of clear targets, and the involvement of parents and staff and community. And yet this study warned, first, that none of the eleven schools saw government policy as helpful; and second, that 'the nature of school improvement . . . has yet to be thoroughly understood and measured in a sensible and sensitive way.' Researchers expressed real doubt about whether such schools would succeed in the long term, once the special effort of rescuing them subsided; whether, in any event, there was any prospect of schools generally achieving these exceptional results; and, finally, whether some of those who were being credited with success against the odds had not simply attracted an easier intake of children.

One of those who took part in the eleven studies and who celebrated the achievement of these schools was Professor Peter Mortimore. However, this support for his early work only left him struggling all the harder to persuade the government to understand the rest of the story:

> *Whilst some schools can succeed against the odds, the possibility of them all doing so, year in and year out, still appears remote, given that the long-term patterning of educational inequality has been strikingly consistent throughout the history of public education in most countries . . . We must be aware of the dangers of basing a national strategy for change on the efforts of outstanding*

21

individuals working in exceptional circumstances.

None of which has stopped the government pursuing precisely such a strategy.

THE KILLING OF THE COMPREHENSIVES

15 SEPTEMBER 1999

ONCE UPON A time, in the late 1960s, well-meaning politicians accepted the most progressive idea in the history of British education. They decided to establish a national network of new schools which would deal equally with all children, providing a free secondary education for all students of all backgrounds, without favour of class or ability. They called these new schools 'comprehensives'.

It was an idea with a powerful anger behind it, a disgust at the old two-tiered system in which children were segregated at the age of eleven: those most in need of education were tipped into second-class schools with sparse resources and no sixth forms, while those who were naturally most able were given more resources and their own A-level classes. The second-tier schools were stigmatised, together with their pupils. The fact that middle-class children tended to prosper in this system, while the poor failed, rubbed political salt in the social wound.

Ever since then, this brave new idea has been dogged by controversy. It has been accused of penalising the brightest children, fostering a culture of non-achievement, allowing egalitarian dogma to smother educational opportunity. It has been blamed for the low levels of literacy and numeracy which have left Britain struggling in international league tables. For families with choice, the most trying moral and parental question before them remains whether or not to entrust their children to this once favoured system. The government remains beset by hostile questions about its current performance and its future prospects.

And yet, this long and fevered debate has begged its most important question. The underlying issue is not whether comprehensive schools are good or bad but whether they even exist. There is almost no voice in Britain now to claim that our state system is adequate. But is it a system of comprehensives, or is this a system whose weaknesses have a very different origin? Consider the case of Sheffield. More than any other British city, Sheffield wears its social divisions on its sleeve. Roughly speaking, the working class – with or without work – live in the old housing estates and crumbling red-brick terraces of the north-east, while the affluent middle class live in the green and pleasant suburbs of the south-west, known in the city as the White Highlands. Such a clear separation highlights the social tensions behind the classroom scenes. The city also has relatively few private schools, and so the education game is played almost entirely within the state sector.

This is the tale of two comprehensives. The first is Abbeydale Grange, already described. It is a classic example of a struggling inner-city school, the kind that is often held up as the clearest evidence of the failure of the comprehensive ideal. The second is Silverdale, the jewel in Sheffield's educational crown, a school whose consistently high academic achievements have won it national praise. It is the kind of success story which is often used as a stick to beat those who lag behind in the league tables.

Now go back thirty years, to the dawn of the comprehensive system in Sheffield. The first thing you see is that the picture is flipped on its head. The top school in the city is not Silverdale but Abbeydale Grange, newly created out of three grammar schools. It is a model of old-fashioned order and achievement, with enviable results in O levels and A levels. And Silverdale – well, Silverdale is struggling, because although it now enjoys the title of 'comprehensive' and is acquiring a new sixth form, its reputation is rooted in its history – as a charmless secondary modern, better perhaps than many other secondary moderns, but nonetheless a school for cast-offs.

The second thing you see – the really important thing – is

the start of a curiously English story. It features a little snobbery, a dash of racism (generally unacknowledged) and a great deal of class politics. It begins here, with the two schools setting out on their journey towards equality, it unfolds over the next thirty years, and it ends with a nasty twist in its tale.

In the beginning, of course, neither school was comprehensive in anything but name, and for several years there was very little change. Each school continued in the inertia of its old reputation: Abbeydale Grange was still a posh school, attracting the children of the middle classes; Silverdale was still for those local middle-class children who were less likely to prosper academically. But by the early 1980s, something new was happening. The intake of each school was evolving.

Abbeydale Grange's new catchment area cut a slice out of some of the most deprived streets in Sheffield. The school was no longer protected by the high fence of the Eleven Plus exam, and the city council had been encouraging 'ordinary people' to enrol. The children of poor families began to turn up in the playground. Some of them were black. A few of the white middle-class parents made it plain that they did not like this and their children left. By the early 1980s, the school's numbers had fallen from 2,300 to less than 2,000. However, most were insulated from these new arrivals by the school's system of setting, which meant that only the brightest of the new arrivals entered the classrooms of the white middle class.

The city council, however, were concerned to help the children of their constituents who complained that they were being pushed into the bottom sets and streams of the old 'posh' schools. They started to push for the adoption of mixed-ability teaching: the poor and the rich, the slow and the bright would be taught together. A lot of teachers objected. They were overruled. More white middle-class families pulled out. The numbers at Abbeydale Grange declined a little more.

In the background, the child population nationally had been falling, but Labour councils like Sheffield (led by one D. Blunkett under the slogan Socialism In One City) had made a pact with the teacher unions whose influence had grown as the old industrial unions collapsed: there were to be no teacher redundancies. The result was that schools were bloated with spare capacity, and although the city did its best to arrange balanced intakes of students, parents from a school like Abbeydale Grange found it easy to transfer their children to a 'quieter' school in an affluent white suburb, a school like Silverdale.

Freed from its second-class status by the removal of the Eleven Plus, bolstered by its new sixth form, Silverdale had slowly become the natural home for more of the children in its middle-class neighbourhood. With its new intake of well-motivated and well-supported children scoring strongly in O levels and A levels, its reputation began to climb. It filled its spare places. Abbeydale, however, with its classrooms beginning to admit the children of the poor, who were tethered by disadvantage, saw its reputation fade. The retreat of the white middle class picked up pace until, by 1985, there were only 1,500 children on the roll.

At this stage, fifteen years into their new identity, two points were clear. First, neither school had yet developed a comprehensive intake. Second, the changing fortunes of the two schools had nothing to do with their educational methods. This was still a time when government and local education authorities funded schools and left it for them to decide how to behave. Unpestered and unsupervised, each school had continued to teach much as it always had. At Abbeydale Grange, the same head teacher, W.J. Grenville Massey, had run the school in the same orthodox fashion for the first thirteen years of its comprehensive life. And yet one school had started to decline while the other had started to thrive – simply because the middle class had started shifting their support from one to the other.

Thus far, however, the change had been slow, an almost unconscious social shift. Now, in the late 1980s, this smouldering burst into flames, as the Tories in the Department of Education intervened.

First, Sir Keith Joseph played a hand. In search of savings, Sheffield City Council had decided to close all the sixth forms in the city and to create in their stead tertiary colleges. Sir Keith, however, was lobbied by parents from the White Highlands, and he ruled that, while schools in the rest of the city might lose their sixth forms, those in the south-west – which happened to elect the only Tory MP in the city – should keep theirs. It was a moment of complete reversal. Silverdale, which as a secondary modern had had no sixth form, now kept its A-level students: they were role models for the younger students, they supported better science labs and language labs, they brought prestige to the school. Abbeydale Grange, once the plump and well-fed grammar school, lost its sixth form and was now officially and visibly a second-rank school.

Then Kenneth Baker took over as education secretary. In a volley of changes, led by the 1988 Education Reform Act, he created a market in state schooling. The education authorities lost the power to assign children to schools; parents alone would choose. The schools would test their children, the results would be published in league tables, which would have a powerful influence on this parental choice. The schools which attracted the most children would be rewarded with extra funds: the vast bulk of the budget of each school would now be decided simply by the number of students on its roll. A flood of change swept through Sheffield.

By this time, South Yorkshire's steel and coal industries had been torn to ribbons by Thatcherism. Unemployment climbed. The property market collapsed. Asian immigrants moved in to the disintegrating inner city and the north-east of Sheffield, and sent their children to the local schools. There was a surge of anxiety about falling academic standards and a new wave of old-fashioned racial hostility. Abbeydale Grange suddenly found itself the scene of a full-scale white exodus. Now there was nothing slow or unconscious about it: by the early 1990s the school which had once boasted 2,300 pupils had been abandoned by almost all the white middle class and was left with fewer than 500 pupils. In the White Highlands, Silverdale was booming.

In theory it was open to the children of the poor families in the north-east to make the same move. This had never been easy. Children from the north-east who were bright enough for the posh grammar schools in the south-west had always felt trapped behind a social barrier. But now, the freedom of choice which the government offered in one hand was removed with the other. The Department for Education ordered cuts. Across the country, local education authorities were instructed to improve the productivity of their schools by slashing their spare capacity. Sheffield lost more than thirty primary and secondary schools. The spare places vanished and were replaced by rules – adopted by almost every LEA – which stipulated that if too many children applied for one school, places would be open to those who lived closest to the school and to those who had siblings there.

Middle-class parents fled from Abbeydale Grange and bought their way in to Silverdale's catchment area. No poor family from the north-east could afford to buy houses there. These children there were left to make do with their struggling local schools. All parents could choose, but some could choose more effectively than others.

Now, the two schools were almost completely polarised in their intake. Dr Phil Budgell, the former chief inspector of schools in Sheffield, analysed census data. His figures revealed that poor children at Abbeydale Grange outnumbered the affluent by more than three to one. Affluent children at Silverdale outnumber the poor by the same factor. Today, Abbeydale Grange has one of the most disadvantaged intakes in the city: 53% of its pupils claim free school meals. At Silverdale, in the White Highlands, only 7% take free meals – less than half the national average. Abbeydale's 45% of pupils with special educational needs compares with fewer than 2% of Silverdale's.

Neither school now is comprehensive in anything but name. Neither school now is any more comprehensive than it was thirty years ago. In those days, the children were selected by examiners. Now, they are selected by estate agents.

This same tide swept through all the state schools in the city. By the time the 1988 Act had completed what the middle class had spontaneously started, Dr Budgell's survey suggested that only five of the twenty-seven secondary schools in the city could claim to have developed a comprehensive intake, with a comparable number of children from both affluent and poor homes. The intake of the other twenty-two

28

was clearly skewed one way or the other, often even more so than that of Abbeydale Grange or Silverdale. Some of the schools in the north-east were swamped by poverty: Fir Vale, for example, had some 55% of its pupils from poor homes and only 11% from affluent; Waltheof had 50% poor and 11% affluent.

Give or take a little local detail, the same story has been told around the country. Northern Ireland has never tried to go comprehensive; Scotland has done so with success, but in England and Wales only a minority of schools has succeeded in becoming comprehensive. Sometimes they are in small towns where there is only one state secondary and not enough social problems to frighten the middle class into private schools; sometimes they have grown through the cracks in big cities, usually by virtue of geographical accident combined with a deliberate policy from the head teacher. But the main story is the same, over and over again.

There are cities which have more private schools than Sheffield and where it is the private sector rather than the suburban state schools which has skimmed off the bright middle-class children. There are cities where the social geography is not as clear as Sheffield's and where mixed areas – like Wandsworth in south London – have introduced 'aptitude tests' to finish the job the local estate agents alone cannot do. The end result is the same. After thirty years of strife, there is a national shortage of comprehensive schools.

And this matters: not simply because the political will of the government thirty years ago has been frustrated; nor even because those schools which are not comprehensive are nevertheless judged as though they were. It matters most of all because this distorted, divisive intake directly jeopardises the educational performance of the schools and the children within them.

The evidence is overwhelming that the single most important factor in a school's performance is its intake: bright children who perform well can lift the performance of others around them. If the bright middle-class children are being siphoned off into private schools and a minority of state schools like Silverdale, then children in the rest of the system will fail to achieve comparable standards. Not because the system is comprehensive. The reverse is true. The system fails because it is segregated, because it leaves the struggling children to struggle alone. In Sheffield, the figures are conclusive. Dr Budgell found that, with small variations, he could take the table which ranked the poverty of the pupil intake, turn it upside down and find himself looking at the table ranking academic success. At Abbeydale Grange in 1998, 22% of the children managed to score at least five A to C grades at GCSE. At Silverdale, 76% did so.

The head teachers at both schools are full of praise for their staff and take pride in their results, but neither of them makes false claims. Abbeydale's results are lifted by a small group of very bright children. The head teacher, Jan Woodhead, said: 'We are very lucky in the sense that we have still got the support of a number of middle-class families, and we keep them because we do a good job for their children.' The head teacher of Silverdale, Helen Storey, is similarly realistic: 'I wouldn't say we are doing something wonderful here that they are not doing at Abbeydale. We do many things in common with other schools to raise attainment. I wouldn't think we are radically different to any other school in that. You are quite likely to achieve more if you have ten per cent difficult children than if you have forty per cent difficult children.'

Here is the truth which almost every teacher knows and almost every politician denies: a school system which becomes as socially polarised as Britain's is guaranteed to generate failure.

And it gets worse. Like a killer left at liberty, the market which was established in 1988 is still out there, stalking the schools. The early damage was done by the combination of cuts and 'parental choice', polarising school catchment areas by house price. But the market has other means of attack, and now, with each year that goes by, the polarisation grows. The key to this is that when the children move, they take the funding with them. The successful school becomes richer; the struggling school becomes poorer. This is more cunning than you might think.

It works like this. In round numbers, under the formula set up by Kenneth Baker, a local government authority will now pay a school, say, £2,000 a year for each child who is enrolled there. Every year, schools compete with each other to attract new eleven-year-olds to start in Year Seven in September. They seek them in blocks of thirty, the maximum which most secondary schools are happy to see in one classroom. The successful school, with its exam results published and acclaimed, can recruit an extra thirty children and bank an extra £60,000. But it does not cost an extra £60,000 to teach the thirty children. Providing it has the classroom space, the school's overheads remain the same. All it has to do is to hire an extra teacher, who might cost about £25,000, and pay a little more for heat and books – a total outlay of no more than £30,000.

The outcome is that the successful school not only expands and funds its expansion but pockets a profit of some £30,000 which it can use to buy more books or computers or spare time for its teachers, all of which may help it to improve its performance, thus generating still better results and more children for the following year. On the other end of the seesaw, the struggling school is pushed further and further down: it loses thirty prospective students and loses £60,000 out of its budget; it can save some money by making a teacher redundant but still it has to find some £30,000 of cuts to balance the budget, thus reducing its chances of lifting its exam results. And every year, the results are published in all their misleading glory, ensuring that the reputations of the schools become a little more polarised, their fortunes a little more divided.

When Jan Woodhead took over as head teacher at Abbeydale Grange in 1994, white flight had left the school insolvent. It was surviving on an accounting muddle: with earlier cuts, they had closed a building, but they were still being paid to heat, light, clean and maintain it. 'The school was dying,' she said. To make matters worse, John Major's government was still squeezing education budgets, and when the more successful schools in Sheffield tried to protect themselves by recruiting extra children, they targeted Abbeydale's possible intake. The school needed at least 120 new children to survive, but in September 1995 the market delivered seventy-three, and the next year only fifty-six. It was the bright children from the aspirational families who were making it through the appeals process to reach the White Highlands. The struggling school was losing the best of its intake, and it was broke.

By 1997, Abbeydale Grange was a quarter of a million pounds in debt. The LEA, recognising that if the school closed it would still have to support these children, came to its rescue with £180,000. The school cut the remaining £70,000 out of its own budget, slashing its management and stretching its teaching staff so severely that within months it had to reverse the cuts in order to keep the school running. Last year, the LEA simply licensed the school to run at a loss. The system does not deliver. Jan Woodhead said: 'The funding formula is based on the concept that you have your basic kid who costs a basic amount of money. Here, that concept has been tested to destruction.'

The struggle goes on. By 1998, Jan Woodhead had re-marketed Abbeydale Grange, turning its loss of pupils to its advantage – 'the small school that makes a big difference' – and celebrating its success at assimilating different cultures. The shortage of places in the rest of the city meant that numerous parents who applied for other schools were given places at Abbeydale. In early summer, the school looked relatively safe, with 154 new children on its list. But, across the city, Silverdale was trying to cope with its own funding crisis by increasing its Year Seven intake from 150 to 180. Twenty-nine families had appealed against their Abbeydale places, asking to go to Silverdale. In search of funds, Silverdale decided not to contest any of the appeals. By the beginning of September, Abbeydale had lost all twenty-nine children to its more successful competitor. To make the injury worse, Abbeydale was already committed to hiring enough teachers for 150 children. More money lost.

In 1999, Silverdale publicly announced that it would not repeat the lawful robbery and agreed to recruit only 150 new students. Nevertheless, the system did the damage. The LEA allowed 162 students to claim places at Silverdale, assuming that some would drop out before September. They had underestimated the extent of the polarisation: parents were not just opting for Silverdale, they were investing all their hopes in it. Not one student dropped out. Then twenty-three others who had been denied places appealed, and four lived close enough to Silverdale to win. So the school had 166 new students – too many for five classrooms, not enough for six. The LEA agreed that if Silverdale still had 166 children on its list in September, they would pay for an extra classroom to house them. And if that happened, there would be spare capacity for fourteen more children – so more of the appeals which had been lost would be reversed. And so it is that in September 1999 Silverdale once more emerged from the muddle of the market with 180 new pupils, while at the other end of the ladder Abbeydale Grange once more lost its new recruits.

At Silverdale, head teacher Helen Storey offered no defence for the system: 'I phoned Jan Woodhead at Abbeydale. She's spitting feathers – "All these kids are going to come from me." I'm not happy with it either. It's not managing the situation effectively. This awful polarisation is really very unhelpful.'

The market has one more weapon with which to bludgeon the weak and wounded – academic cleansing. Some head teachers are so anxious for their schools to shine in the league tables that they get rid of students who are likely to perform badly in exams. They can do this by illegally denying the difficult child a place: all they have to do is to claim that they are full, and nobody checks. Or, if the child is already inside their classrooms, they can formally exclude them, but that makes the school look bad. And so, in secret, they cleanse them: they call in the student's parents, warn them their child is about to be excluded, and let them remove the child voluntarily. This not only rids the school of the difficult pupil without registering an exclusion, it also allows the cleansing school to keep the income from that child until their pupil numbers are next officially counted. 'It is illegal and immoral,' according to one head teacher, 'but it is also quite widespread.'

On the other end of the cleansing is a struggling school which has vacancies and cannot refuse to take a displaced child. In this way Abbeydale Grange, already struggling with a high proportion of difficult children, last year received sixty more students, most of them with a track record of disorder and disruption, many of whom arrived without bringing a single penny of funding with them. In the black market in unwanted children, a struggling school is a big buyer.

All state schools complain they are short of money. In Sheffield even Silverdale, with its booming intake, is running on a deficit of £170,000 a year. If they balanced their budget, they say, they would have to close their sixth form or slash the curriculum. It has no spare staff, it is desperately short of facilities. It houses drama in a temporary classroom which is rotting so badly that they can use it only occasionally. Helen Storey said: 'The system is so underfunded that everybody has some inequality to deal with.'

But the schools with disadvantaged children are in an even worse state. Apart from losing cash as their results fall, they are dealing with a disproportionate number of children with special educational needs. In theory, these bring with them not just the standard funding but also some extra money. In practice, the Department of Education distributes funds for Additional Educational Needs according to a formula which notoriously undershoots its target. Schools are also given grants for a few children whose needs are so great that they are 'statemented' for help from a group of agencies. This money can pay for a support assistant to work directly with the child. The trouble is that schools have started to apply for so many children to be statemented that LEAs like Sheffield have imposed a ceiling on the amount of money they will pay out, regardless of the need the schools declare. Jan Woodhead said: 'The money you get for a child with special educational needs is never enough to fund the provision you have to make.'

At Abbeydale the roof leaks, the drama department has no lights, the cricket team no pitch, the model pyramids in the maths room are made of rolled-up newspaper, ancient fire damage still scars the wall of the science room, last term's trip to Alton Towers was cancelled because there were no staff to take it, the boiler is broken, the driveway is crumbling, and, most important, there is a constant, nagging shortage of cash for staff. The head teacher is working an eighty-four-hour week to hold it together. 'Our finances are surreal,' said Jan Woodhead. 'We're just not solvent.'

The point of all this is not just that schools need a fairer system of league tables. The fault goes much deeper. A 'value-added' league table would only shuffle the order of the schools in the table, exposing different schools to the real problem of the system, which is that it attacks the schools who most need help. Very efficiently, the current system identifies those schools which are struggling. It then robs those schools of their brightest pupils and thus of their funds, guaranteeing that their struggle becomes more desperate. The fact that these schools almost without exception are struggling in the first place because they are sited in poor areas with an intake of disadvantaged children means that these extra burdens are placed almost unfailingly on the schools that serve the poor. The converse is also true: those that serve affluent neighbourhoods prosper. And so the school system divides along class lines. It is the very existence of a market which is the problem.

It is all a very long way from the thirty-year-old dream of a network of comprehensive schools. In their place, we have developed a two-tiered system in which the children most in need of education are tipped into second-class schools with sparse resources and no sixth forms, while those who are naturally most able are given more resources and their own A-level classes. The second-tier schools are stigmatised, together with their pupils. The fact that middle-class children tend to prosper in this system while the poor fail, rubs political salt in the social wound.

'It is not standing still. It is getting worse and worse. It is becoming more and more polarised. There is a horrendous backlash going to happen, and yet there is almost a wilful blindness to it.' Jan Woodhead, head teacher at Abbeydale Grange, said that.

'The blunt truth is that Britain is still, after all these years, a place where class counts, where the best do not always come through and whose institutions reinforce a sense of us as a country living in our past, not learning from it.' Tony Blair said that.

Real comprehensives still work

At its root, the idea of a comprehensive school rests on the possibility of using bright middle-class children as an asset for the educational system, to be distributed like fertiliser to help the poorer children grow. But does it work?

The clearest evidence was captured by researchers at Edinburgh University in 1996. They studied comprehensives in Grampian and found: 'The attainment of all pupils in a school is enhanced if the school has many pupils from advantaged backgrounds.' But in the same conclusion, they also pointed to the potential problem: 'Conversely, the attainment of all pupils in a school is depressed if a school has few pupils from advantaged backgrounds.'

From the viewpoint of a middle-class parent, that one conclusion contains both the thrill and the threat of comprehensive schools: the prospect of their bright child either soaring and taking others with it or sinking beneath the weight of other children's disadvantage. For education researchers, it raises a key question – at what point does the mixed composition of a school or a classroom move from being constructive to destructive? This study of the 'compositional effect' lies unarticulated beneath much of the political debate about the future of state schools: the rights and wrongs of selection, the future of grammar schools, the viability of comprehensives.

As the former head of an inner London comprehensive, Margaret Maden has seen this in practice. As the head of the Centre for Successful Schools at Keele, she has studied it. Her conclusion is clear: 'If you have something around twenty to twenty-five per cent in a class or in a school who are well motivated and come from homes where it's instilled in them from very early on that education and learning matter and are fun and make a difference to your life, then that makes the progress with less well-motivated children and families much much easier.

'When you get a concentration of children – you can call them disturbed or disadvantaged – there is a critical mass of children who will wreck any school. I will defy any teacher to teach when you have got more than thirty per cent of kids like that in the school . . . Beyond a certain point children will not succeed educationally if they are concentrated in a school where the majority of children need to be persuaded that education matters.'

Her conclusions are supported not only by the Grampian research but also by a thirty-month project for the Economic and Social Research Council, which examined the results of ninety-four different schools and which also confirmed the educational benefits of a balanced intake. Researchers in New Zealand in 1997 came to the same conclusion. The positive advantage of a balanced intake is stressed by Howard Glennester, Professor of Social Policy at the LSE, who concludes: 'Pupils from "uncreamed" comprehensives do better in examinations than those in selective areas.'

If this is right, then the case for selection or for retaining grammar schools is profoundly weakened, since the creaming off of the brightest 25% actively undermines the academic outcome for the remaining 75%. This selection breaks almost entirely along class lines: in May, the government released figures which showed that selective schools and grammar schools have almost no poor children, with less than 1% of their pupils being entitled to free meals.

And so, for the middle-class parent, the moral agony is increased: as a result of this 'compositional effect', their decision to avoid the failing state school in their area becomes an active ingredient in that school's failure. And yet, for as long as their middle-class neighbours continue to avoid the school, their lone child could struggle if the school's intake remains unbalanced. The real problem is that the decision now has to be made amid a national shortage of comprehensives, caused originally by middle-class flight and now institutionalised by the reforms of the late 1980s in a system which tends overwhelmingly to produce the wrong mixture of children in our classrooms.

AN EDUCATION SECRETARY CONFESSES

16 SEPTEMBER 1999

LORD BAKER IS laughing. He is recalling all the dark suspicions he aroused when he ran the Department of Education in the late 1980s. He dismissed them at the time as the whining of an establishment that couldn't cope with change, and he went ahead and rewrote the rule book for Britain's schools – SATs tests, league tables, national curriculum, parental choice, local management of schools, and later Ofsted. The system David Blunkett runs today was designed by Kenneth Baker ten years ago.

He knows a lot of people tried to say that he was really just settling political scores, that his real agenda was to punish the teacher unions and to kill off the local education authorities, and that secretly the big master plan was to wipe out comprehensive schools by stealth. And now he's laughing because the funny thing is – they were right!

Lord Baker lives in an eye-wateringly beautiful house in one of the prettiest villages in Sussex. He sits in his armchair in the corner of his comfortable study, surrounded by piles of books and the political cartoons he collects, and he grins as he tells the inside story of what really happened after Margaret Thatcher told him in May 1986 that Something Had To Be Done about the schools.

It is a revealing story. On the face of it, a reform of schools would have to have, as its overriding priority, the welfare of children. And since this involved the construction of a new system to disseminate learning and knowledge, it would have to be built on a particularly strong intellectual foundation, a great deal of solid research and clear thinking. Not so. The most sweeping educational reforms this century, it transpires, had just as much to do with guesswork, personal whim and bare-knuckle politics.

And that, in turn, is part of a wider and more alarming paradox: that the politics of education are built on foundations of ignorance. There are core questions which have never been answered. Sometimes this is because there is a shortage of hard information: how do children learn; what is the best age to begin schooling; should children sit exams at sixteen? Sometimes it is because the answers are moral and not factual: should you promote the education of the slow at the expense of the bright; are we delivering education for its own sake or for the sake of the economy; is it acceptable for the children of the rich to buy better schools? This vacuum of understanding frequently is filled by political ideology.

When he took over, Lord Baker says, education really was an awful mess. For a start, the teachers had been on a rolling strike for nearly eighteen months: 'You can't overestimate the importance of that strike.' Particularly because it made him very angry. He had seen it spreading while he was at the Department of Environment, he had watched the unions digging in their heels. 'It was impossible with the unions – endless meetings, getting nowhere, all fighting against each other.' When Margaret Thatcher moved him to Education, he decided to deal with them. His first move was quite open. He cut off their muscle.

'I took away all negotiating rights from the union. It was quite brutal.' He chuckles drily in his armchair as he recalls how by statute he removed their right to negotiate and set up an advisory committee which would simply set the rates of teacher pay on its own. 'It was absolutely extreme stuff. Ah-huh-huh-huh.' But he wanted more than that, and his next attack was more subtle. It was aimed not just at the teacher unions but also at the local education authorities. He had developed a deep antipathy towards both of them, because, he says, they had a political agenda.

The Inner London Education Authority had killed off a grammar school in his old Marylebone constituency – 'sheer vandalism'. He remembers being horrified on some official visit, to see primary school children being taught to play a game called Bosses and Workers. 'It was building in conflict. Unbelievable.' Now it was ILEA's turn to be killed off. And the LEAs generally – 'I wanted them to wither on the vine.' They did nothing for parents, he says. They were forcing pupils to go to some truly second-rate schools, simply to protect the jobs of the teachers there. On the basis of this personal experience, he built his policy. 'I think they were behaving in a way that was so damaging to the process of education that I had to remove their power.' He decided to legislate to introduce the Local Management of Schools (LMS).

This had started as a purely educational project. His predecessor, Sir Keith Joseph, had been researching LMS, trying to discover what would happen to schools if head teachers and governors were allowed to control their own budgets, thus giving them far more power over every aspect of school life. Lord Baker was interested in the research but he was also interested in the politics. LMS would fragment the teacher unions by giving them thousands of different employers to deal with and no chance of collective bargaining, and it would rob the LEAs of their most powerful function by taking their hand out of the till: 'I legislated for LMS,' he says, with his eyes gleaming behind his glasses, 'and it diminished the power of the teacher unions and the LEAs. They hate me. Ah-huh-huh-huh.' Whether the quality of education was improved by LMS is less clear.

And he was not yet finished with the LEAs. He went on to give parents the right to choose their child's school, thus robbing the LEAs of their second most important function, the allocation of pupils. From the safety of retirement he now makes no secret of his ulterior motive. 'Oh, certainly there was a political edge to the attack on the LEAs. Oh, yes, though no one ever admitted it. But then they had a political agenda, too. The unions and the LEAs had got the system stitched up, the parents were just there. It was a huge producer-led cartel.'

If he had had the time, he would have done more. 'I would

have reduced the LEAs to dealing with special educational needs and not much else.' But time was limited and he believed he had done enough. He grins like a B-movie bad guy: 'I put them on the course to slowly wither on the vine.' He makes no apology for this. 'I have no regrets. My sins are of omission rather than commission.' He means he would like also to have slipped a stiletto into the professors of education – 'all part of the same cartel'.

The introduction of parental choice was part of a much bigger silent coup. His real target, he says, was the comprehensive system of schooling itself. 'I would have liked to bring back selection, but if I did it, I would have got into such controversy at an early stage that the other reforms would have been lost.' But did he realise that the introduction of 'parental choice' would polarise the system and effectively kill off the comprehensives? 'Oh, yes. That was deliberate. In order to make changes, you have to come from several points.' He had already tried to break things up by introducing the City Technical Colleges and promoting Grant-Maintained Schools: 'Choice was the other weapon.'

The political appeal was simple: choice means freedom, and freedom is good. But the real objective was a lot more destructive. 'I hoped it would open it all up and it would lead to the poorer schools literally having to close.' Stealth was essential. 'I was not going to take on the comprehensive system head-on. I'd had the teachers' strike, the national curriculum, you can't take on yet another great fight. So I believed that if I set in train certain changes, that they would have, er, a cumulative beneficial effect. Ah-huh-huh-huh.'

At first, he had wanted to undermine the system by introducing a formal voucher system, where parents could spend their 'education voucher' on the school of their choice, starving unpopular schools of funding. His predecessor, Sir Keith Joseph, had first floated the plan, but he had been thrown off the scent by Whitehall's mandarins. 'I loved Keith dearly, Keith was a lovely person, but he was seduced by very clever civil servants in the department. I had a much more practical approach. I could see the advantage of a voucher system, but Heath and a lot of the Conservative Party were against them.' So he couldn't do it. At least, not openly.

Instead, he combined parental choice with his new funding formula, which meant that the vast bulk of each school's budget depended entirely on the recruitment of children, whose parents were now empowered to choose their schools. 'Well, yes, it's not a formal voucher system, but it's very tantamount! Ah-huh-huh-huh. In effect, it was a voucher system. I just didn't call it that. It was a subtler approach. Ah-huh-huh-huh.'

The attack on the comprehensives worked. Baker's legacy, as we have shown, is a national shortage of comprehensive schools. His reforms polarised the entire system between schools which gather the brightest children and the most funds and which are effectively grammar schools; and the contemporary equivalent of secondary modern schools, invariably in poor areas, where there is a concentration of disadvantaged children struggling for education on a reduced budget. This has helped the middle class, whose children tend to fill the classrooms of the successful schools, but it has abandoned the poor. While the number of bright children scoring five A to Cs has risen steadily, the same 10 or 11% of disadvantaged children still leave school at sixteen without a single qualification to their name. The attack on the teacher unions and the LEAs also succeeded, though the LEAs may yet flower again on their vine. And this whole shift was achieved with barely a supporting fact behind it. Politically, it was brilliant. Educationally, it was a hoax.

Lord Baker may laugh, but it is striking how many of his reforms were rooted in whim. He says that when he took over from Sir Keith Joseph there was no grand plan. 'Keith was very nice and helpful and left me a list of ten problem areas. They were all quite obvious, just bush fires really that were always raging – not enough money for books and so on. But there was no blueprint.' Mrs Thatcher had simply told him to go away for a month or two and come up with something. So he did.

He says he was well aware of the powerful body of expert opinion that a school full of poor children would always struggle academically, but, he says, he saw through that when

43

he went to New York in 1987 and visited a primary school in the Bronx. 'There was barbed wire everywhere, they were frisking the kids. It was unbelievable.' And he watched a group of seven-year-olds act the witches' scene from *Macbeth*. 'That brought home to me that with really great teaching, you can overcome social disadvantages,' he says, although he concedes that 'they didn't know where Scotland was or who Macbeth was, but they knew what witches were.'

His decision to use parental choice and the funding formula to create a market in school places was a seismic shift. What made him think that a market would help the education of children? What was the model? What was the country whose experience encouraged him? Where was the research? The answer is that there was just about none. He thinks there might have been some American research, possibly from that man Charles Murray. Certainly, however, there was politics: political ideology, pumped in particular from the Centre for Policy Studies, which said that markets were A Good Thing; and there was Kenneth Baker's political agenda.

He introduced the network of City Technical Colleges (CTCs), funded by business. 'Everybody attacked them, Conservative as well as Labour – "regressive", "not needed".' He says the truth is that the idea for them came from a visit he made years earlier to a project under some railway arches somewhere, where he saw unqualified school-leavers working enthusiastically on computers. And he thought it was wonderful, and so at the DTI he set up a few IT Education Centres and then he launched the whole network of CTCs. No, there wasn't any research behind them. Although they did have the advantage of being set up outside the power of the LEAs. Ah-huh-huh-huh.

The result of this kind of approach is a system which has been a complete political success but which now saps the strength of struggling schools by taking away their brightest pupils and some of their funds. It is an ambiguous legacy. The underlying point is that in a sense he shares it with his Labour counterparts, before and since: they too substituted ideology for understanding in a debate which has been poisoned by politics.

Nigel de Gruchy, leader of the NAS/UWT and one of the most outspoken critics of Baker's reforms, can see the same kind of politicisation in past Labour reforms: 'The 1970s reforms were driven entirely by lecturers and education directors and politically motivated union leaders. During the 1980s, Labour local authorities used the teacher unions as a battering ram against the Tory government.'

There are teachers now who shake their heads in embarrassment at the memory of the days when they refused to mark their students' work for fear of criticising them; or when they rewrote the curriculum to take account of their belief that they were all racist imperialists; or when they taught the children educational games about bosses and workers. In the same way, councillors and LEA officials now marvel at the way that schools were simply funded and left to get on with it with very little supervision and no interference.

Peter Horton, who was chair of education in Sheffield before David Blunkett's era, looks back now with anxiety: 'There was a very great complacency about accountability and standards. There were half a dozen really useless head teachers, and there was nothing that could be done about it. And nobody was trying. The officials used to say: "We are here to save souls, not to damn them".' It is true, as Lord Baker complains, that in Sheffield, as elsewhere, local authorities protected the jobs of teachers even where there was no demand for them: one Sheffield school, Park House, is said to have had enough staff for 1,200 children even though in reality it had only 400.

Now, once again, as the Blair government attempts to lift standards, the political is interfering with the educational. The new Social Exclusion Unit (SEU), which is mapping the campaign against poverty, has delivered only one report on schools, dealing with truancy and exclusion. It was a thorough and honest piece of work. Its authors recognised that Ken Baker's system has given schools an incentive to play dirty, to refuse to admit difficult children, to exclude them or 'cleanse' them, all of which results in their being dumped into struggling schools that cannot turn them away. The SEU recognised that one way to deal with this was to remove the pressure from the schools by challenging the whole idea of parental choice and the funding formula. But they didn't. They made no mention at all of this implication of their work. Why? 'It was so sensitive,' according to a senior figure in the Unit, 'so politically sensitive, we just left it alone.'

That particular political compromise is part of a much wider political judgement – to leave the Baker reforms in place. Their effect in undermining the comprehensive system and in condemning struggling schools to even greater struggles may be mourned at the most senior levels in the Department for Education, but the consensus is that they cannot 'go back and fight the *Daily Mail*'.

David Blunkett has moved to help struggling schools in a way that his Conservative predecessors entirely abjured. He has announced an extra £19 billion of schools funding, which is being parcelled out into a mass of initiatives and projects. He is pushing through a whole raft of proposals under the title 'Excellence in Cities'. He is creating Education Action Zones (EAZs) where schools can find extra funds and a freedom to improvise. At the moment, the jury is out on the merits of all this. There are those who criticise his efforts, who say that the EAZs and the Private Finance Initiatives are gravitating towards the more successful schools; that he has created a 'bidding culture' in which weak schools are unlikely to do well and in which too much money is devoted to sideshows such as breakfast clubs and adult literacy schemes, while the core lack of funding is left untouched. There are senior figures in Ofsted who worry privately that he is rearranging structures without effecting standards, an exercise in educational window-dressing. Head teachers say they are getting lost in a blizzard of initiatives and that the whole system is now 'ludicrously overmanaged'. Against all this, Blunkett can claim that exam results continue to improve and that his efforts with disadvantaged children dwarf those of his predecessors.

Time will tell whether the critics are right or not. However, the greater problem is that, as long as Lord Baker's system remains untouched, all of David Blunkett's reforms are being fed into a structure which constantly penalises the schools he is attempting to help. It is as if he too has been suckered by Lord Baker's sleight of hand. This is the education secretary who promised 'No selection – read my lips' but who has bought a second-hand system which is selective in all but name.

You can see the strain in the system as David Blunkett's department struggles to put up its little tent in the howling gale of Lord Baker's reforms, desperately trying to lash everything together with more and more central command: action plans, school development plans, LEA education development plans, target setting, benchmarking, naming and shaming, appraisal, baseline assessment, self-assessment, national assessment, records of achievement, best value studies, Ofsted inspections, pre-Ofsted inspections, LEA inspections. And still, Lord Baker's market wins.

There may yet be a twist in this tale of politicised thinking. The most potent force in the politics of education over the last fifty years has been the middle-class parents. The grammar schools were created for them. When their children started finding themselves in secondary moderns, the comprehensives were created for them instead. (The Queen of Comprehensives, the education secretary who created more than any other, was not Shirley Williams but Margaret Thatcher.) When they fled from that system, Kenneth Baker gave them parental choice. But now there are signs that Baker's system is letting them down, too. Cuts have reduced spare capacity. We are about to see a demographic bulge in the number of children of secondary school age. More middle-class parents are being driven to the expense of the private sector, or to distant selective state schools, or to schools that foster a religion in which they have no real faith. More of them are simply failing to find schools they like. The Adult Commission estimates that 20% of parents now fail to get their first choice of secondary school.

The middle class may yet desert the Labour Education Secretary who has done so much to try to reassure them. From the comfort of his armchair, Lord Baker looks at David Blunkett's agenda – more homework, more parental

47

involvement, more discipline: 'He seems to have recycled a lot of my speeches. Ah-huh-huh-huh.'

Chris Woodhead's world of phoney facts

They really don't know. The world of education is rather like the world of the Fortean Times, *'The Journal of Strange Phenomena'. A few years ago, the magazine totted up the number of reports they had been sent from around the world that year describing bizarre and inexplicable events. They compared the total with the number of similar reports received the previous year involving various freaks and flying saucers and concluded triumphantly that the world had become 3.5% weirder.*

The difference, however, between the world of education and the Fortean Times *is that the journal of strange phenomena has its tongue in its cheek. The civil servants and academics and pundits who inform the most important domestic debate in the country may produce findings which have no statistical validity at all, and yet they present them with a straight face, claiming to have uncovered the truth, when the alarming reality very often is that they really don't know.*

In summer 1999, for example, the chief inspector of schools, Chris Woodhead, wrote an acidic essay in the Independent *flaying 'elitist liberals' who disagreed with the Education Secretary's views on homework. In support of his position, Woodhead wrote: 'When I became chief inspector five years ago, twenty to thirty per cent of lessons were routinely judged by inspectors to be unsatisfactory or poor ... Now, more than 50% of lessons taught to seven to eleven year olds are routinely judged to be good.' Point made. But look again.*

There are several problems here. The smallest problem is that in 1994, when Woodhead took over, Ofsted had gathered so little data from its new work in primary schools that it published no figures at all for them in its annual report. Ofsted's chief press officer confirms that the database simply was not big enough to produce any reliable results. If

Woodhead has not simply invented the figures, he may be ignoring the paucity of data and relying on a crude table from the time which does show a failure rate of the kind he reports; if that is his source, he fails to tell his readers that this crude table also suggested that more than 40% of the relevant lessons were rated good or very good.

More important, however, is the fact that the entire basis of the comparison is invalid because since 1994 the methods of inspection, the criteria of measurement and the number of grades have all changed. The hopelessness of making this kind of comparison was put powerfully by one education expert who was apparently frustrated at the abuse of Ofsted evidence:

'In 1996, the framework for inspection was revised and significant changes were made to the way in which lessons are graded by inspectors and the way in which standards achieved by pupils are judged. In addition there were some changes in the criteria used by inspectors to judge other aspects of the quality and efficiency of schools. While this has improved the quality of inspection, it makes precise comparisons with previous years impossible.'

Impossible? The man who wrote that was Chris Woodhead, in his 1996/7 annual report. Fortean indeed.

Despite the impossibility of making these year-on-year comparisons, Chris Woodhead and government ministers regularly use Ofsted data to do so. If it is beguiling for the public, it is infuriating for Ofsted's inspectors, who have queued up (in private) to complain. 'There is a real shortage of hard data,' according to one of them. 'We cannot give a hard answer. All we can do is to take a view. The government is being told stupid things.'

Tory ministers, for example, supported by Woodhead, seized on figures which appeared to show that smaller class sizes did nothing to yield better academic results. This was a powerful statistic, since it struck at the heart of left-wing criticism and potentially saved the Treasury an enormous bill for extra teachers. Unfortunately, the figures are Fortean from *start to finish. In the current market in education, struggling schools lose pupils and so they have smaller classes. But they were struggling in the first place because they had so many disadvantaged children. Those who leave tend to be the bright, middle-class children whose parents can afford to move house and can negotiate the appeals procedure. And so they leave behind them a school which has small classes, populated by children who do badly in exams. On the other side of the tracks, the successful school fills up its classrooms with bright children, who turn in good results. Did Chris Woodhead not understand that? As one of his Ofsted inspectors told the* Guardian: *'The correlation is entirely bogus.'*

Chris Woodhead has launched scathing attacks on teachers who run their classes in small groups. In support of his claim that 'whole-class teaching' generates better results and is now used far more frequently than in the past, he likes to refer to Ofsted's own unpublished data and to the work of Maurice Galton at Leicester University. However, when pressed, Ofsted told us in writing that they had no such data to support the claim, and Maurice Galton said he did not agree with Woodhead's position. He says that no one really understands what makes a good teacher and that, contrary to Woodhead's claim of an increase in whole-class teaching: 'What teachers do with children has not changed – only what is taught has changed. The whole of twenty years effort has not changed anything of the fundamental structure in the classroom.'

Fortean statistics are riddled like woodworm through the structure of the debate on education. Sometimes it is a question of clashing statistics, as with the noisy squabble this summer [1999] about whether primary school children should do half an hour's homework each evening. David Blunkett said they should, but researchers at Durham University said better results were achieved by children who did less homework. Blunkett's people poured scorn on them. The Durham people replied that Blunkett had done no research. Blunkett's people say Yes, they had, and that it was the Durham people who had not done their homework properly. The truth is that they really don't know.

More often, it is a matter of misreading the statistics that are available. Chris Woodhead famously claims there are 15,000 incompetent teachers. Some of his inspectors disagree. 'I write the reports he's reading,' said one. 'He can say that n% of lessons are judged to be less than satisfactory. That does not entitle him to say that n% of teachers are incompetent. That's a very different thing. A competent teacher can have an unsatisfactory lesson. Plus it is subjective, this data we provide is impressionistic. And it shouldn't be used for the drawing of these bogus, politically acceptable tabloid slogans.'

Ofsted justifies its own role by pointing out that since it started work, in 1992/3, there has been a steady rise in the number of pupils scoring at least five A to Cs at GCSE. But wait. Look at Scotland, where Ofsted has no role to play: the comprehensive schools there have seen their GCSE results rising just as fast and, lately, even faster. Or look at Northern Ireland: no comprehensives, no Ofsted, but the same annual rise in results. Or consider the fact that the exam results of sixteen-year-olds in England started rising relentlessly in 1980, more than ten years before Ofsted started work. What does it mean? That some other factor is driving up the performance of children – more pressure to find work, more access to information, better teaching even? Or is it just that the examiners keep moving the goalposts to make it easier for the students to score? They really don't know.

In a lecture in February 1998, Chris Woodhead told his audience: 'Down on the bedrock, the crusade for higher standards involves a clash of ideologies which will be resolved not by the intrusion of political will but by the exercise of a quality which is in rather shorter supply: intellectual clarity.' Just so.

THE DEBATE
David Blunkett replies

It doesn't take 15,000 words of *Guardian* prose to tell me or anyone else brought up in one of the most disadvantaged areas of Britain that there is a big divide between the haves and the have-nots in education. As secretary of state, I am acting to overcome it.

Yesterday, Tony Blair and I visited Southfield school in Luton. It is not in a well-off area: more than 30% of its pupils receive free school meals, well over the national average of 17%, and it has a diverse school population representing the ethnic mix of Luton.

Yet the proportion of 11-year-olds getting good results has risen dramatically since 1997 – up 16% in maths to 60% this year, and up 20% in English to 64%. This is no accident. It demonstrates some realities about the government's approach to education, which were virtually ignored by Nick Davies this week.

Southfield has a dynamic head teacher, Marilyn Redfern, who has turned around a school which was failing. A good head makes a big difference regardless of where a school is located. A strong, dynamic head teacher is vital to success – so is a committed team of teachers with high expectations of what can be achieved. That is why we are developing a new college of school leadership and pressing ahead with better rewards for good teachers.

More than two years ago, when we acknowledged that there were schools which had been failing too long, we faced much criticism. Yet admitting to failure is the first step to remedying it. Had we just named and shamed, the criticism might have been justified. But we did rather more than that.

We insisted that any school that had been failing for more than two years had to have a fresh start – with a new head and school team, maybe a new name too – or be closed and its pupils transferred to better schools. We actively worked with those schools which had been left to drift by Conservative inaction. It now takes seventeen months on average to turn around a failing school compared with twenty-five months in

52

1997 – and the number of schools in special measures fell last school year for the first time.

Of course, our education policy is backed by substantial extra resources. The extra £19bn over three years is real – and means an extra £200 per pupil after inflation compared with an £80 real terms cut in the last three Tory budgets. It has already allowed us to repair 10,000 schools as part of a £5bn programme. Four thousand extra primary teachers this term are helping cut infant class sizes. Four times as many primary schools are linked to the internet this year than last. Sure Start and 40,000 more free nursery places for three-year-olds are already giving many youngsters a more equal start in life.

We spend significant sums on tackling social exclusion in inner-city schools such as Abbeydale Grange in Sheffield. From this month, our £350m 'excellence in cities' programme will mean that in inner-city secondary schools, there will be a programme to stretch the most able pupils as well as learning mentors to work with those most at risk of disaffection – modernising comprehensive education. Abbeydale Grange is enthusiastically participating in excellence in cities.

New learning centres in these areas will provide greater access to IT and other facilities, just as the rapid expansion of specialist schools is lifting standards and boosting resources for the wider community. One in four secondary schools, many in the inner cities, will have a specialism by 2002 – results are rising twice as fast in non-selective specialist schools as in other comprehensives. By enabling pupils aged 14 and upwards who would otherwise truant to spend part of the week with a work-related curriculum and by addressing attendance and behaviour problems one-to-one and early (with on-site units in those schools where discipline gets out of hand) we are doing much to overcome the problems faced by inner-city secondaries.

The Tories were content to write off 40% of primary children. We are not. Already this government has begun to transform our primary schools – yesterday showed how we are getting the basics right. Last September, schools in England started the literacy hour, a structured approach to learning English, which recognises the importance of phonics, ensures that pupils learn spelling, punctuation and grammar – and offers more opportunities to study poetry, prose, drama and literature than ever before. Nationally, it has led to a 5% improvement in English results at eleven, with even bigger improvements in reading standards.

Our critics claim that the strategy – and its sister strategy for maths – has been a centralising burden on schools. Yet 70% of schools chose to start the numeracy strategy last year, resulting in a 10% improvement in maths results at eleven. Others started this month. There is still much work to be done in improving standards, but the results are a huge tribute to the teachers, their pupils and parents. They have not taken the route of cynicism or despair. Their 'can do' attitude is a welcome breath of fresh air.

It is also a strong antidote to Nick Davies, who implies that we should wring our hands in despair and accept that you can't expect poor kids to do better (or otherwise, presumably, he would have us marching or busing middle-class kids from the suburbs into the inner cities as he abolishes parental rights).

I have never pretended that, in general, schools with a poorer intake don't perform less well than those with a better off intake. What I don't accept is that we should have lower expectations on the basis of class – and this year's test results show it. It does mean extra resources – and we spend a lot more on pupils in schools in disadvantaged areas than in the rest of the country. But we must target that spending too.

What was heartening about the results this week is that results have improved more than the average (and they needed to do so) in many inner-city areas. In Rotherham, maths rose 14%, English by 9%. In Sheffield, maths was up 12% and English 6%. In Redcar, it was 13% in maths, 9% in English.

I have never underestimated the challenge we are facing. We had good news from our primaries yesterday – showing we are on the right track – and we will want to see big improvements in our urban comprehensives.

In tomorrow's Britain, we cannot afford to write off any child, just because our school system doesn't fit neatly into preconceived notions of ideological correctness – whether they be of the right or left. But this is a challenge which we must all work together to meet if we are to prepare Britain educationally, socially and economically for the new century.

Guardian *readers, join the debate*

Since April I have been working as an 'appropriate adult' in Sheffield attending children who have been arrested. Nick Davies has described exactly the appalling social conditions that are endured day in, day out by virtually all of the 'young offenders' I meet in the custody suites. The only thing I would add is that not only parents are often clinically depressed. Of the children I have seen, at least 50% have demonstrated symptoms of depression – withdrawn, low self-esteem, poor concentration, truancy, loneliness, mood swings, self-harming, suicidal thoughts.

Schools in Sheffield are struggling valiantly in the face of impossible odds because no government has had the courage to take on board what Nick Davies has described and many of us have known for years; that poverty, social deprivation and exclusion are at the root of so many schools' apparent failure to achieve in the 'success' league tables.
Lesley Boulton
Sheffield

Confirmation of Nick Davies's analysis can also be found in the structure of the Panda report (Performance and Assessment) sent to all schools from Ofsted each year. This report is supposed to allow comparison of each school's academic results with similar schools. The bands they use for comparison of poverty are in terms of free school meals. They are up to 5%, 5–9%, 9–13%, 13–21%, 21–35% and those with more than 35% are all lumped together.

Thus schools with 59% free school meals like ours are judged against schools with 35%, when the level of poverty is clearly vastly different. The fact that the bands get wider as the percentage of free school meals increases stems from a philosophy which totally underestimates the effect of poverty on educational attainment. Or perhaps it's deliberate to justify the 'poverty is no excuse' argument.

Colin Sutherland
Chair of Governors
Ribbleton Hall High School, Preston

Nick Davies is wrong to dismiss the counter-evidence to his argument. There is abundant evidence that education can counter the effects of severe deprivation. Three separate surveys of reading in the US show that the amount and quality of practice is a more reliable indicator of reading achievement than the instructional method used or even the students' socio-economic background.

In a large-scale, independently conducted trial in its Bulwell Education Action Zone, Nottingham City LEA tested children who attended the 100 Days Project homework club. They showed 'astonishing' gains in maths and in English.

Five schools in Nottingham's Bulwell EAZ were volunteered by the LEA as the toughest possible trial of the effectiveness of the project. Over 400 children were tested before the trial began, and again at the end of the ten-week period; the results of the participant group were compared with a control group who did not receive tuition. Over 85% of the children tested scored below the national average in the standardised NFER tests used. Significantly, the situation was reversed only ten weeks later with over 85% of the children receiving tuition scoring above the national average.

These results are significant. First, they show that there are methods that will enable young people to catch up even if they attend schools in the most deprived areas. Second, the approach is designed to be cost-effective and easily transferable (two-thirds of the staff who taught on the EAZ project had not taught on it before).

Education can make a difference even in the face of the worst problems.

John Derbyshire
The 100 Days Project
People's College, Nottingham

Unlike your reporter, I know what Abbeydale Grange School had really been, for I was a student there. To describe the former boys' grammar school, and its sister schools, as pursuing high achievement and 'old-fashioned discipline' begs the question as to how it all went so wrong. Yes, we referred to the masters as 'Sir'; yes, we stood when they entered the classroom and, yes, we handed in our homework on time but, no, we did not have a role in the appointment of staff. Mostly, we worked hard, and played hard. To suggest that the inhabitants of the city's numerous council estates were, somehow, excluded from this by a culture which denigrated education is to cast a slur on the many, myself included, who came from these backgrounds and achieved much academically.

That local parents no longer send their children to the school gives a clue to the real reason for its decline. For this school was, like the other grammar schools in Sheffield, deliberately destroyed, sacrificed on the altar of ideology. The present secretary of state was a member of a council which flew the red flag from the town hall on May day, and engineered comprehensivisation in such a way that levelling down, not up, was the deliberate object of policy. By the early 70s, the head of the newly-merged schools, who had been headmaster of the boys' school in my day, was admitting, in a BBC interview, that parents whose elder children had been students under selection, were expressing concern that their younger children were faring less well.

Finally, lest this be dismissed as the rantings of a middle-aged man looking back with misty eyes at his lost youth, let me point out that I work in the state education sector. I see, daily, the declining standards in our schools, with barely-numerate students entering higher education, and I know that the true story of my old school is a metaphor for the present sad state.
John Taylor
Ashford, Kent

As an ex-pupil of Abbeydale Grammar School, and as head teacher of a junior school in a disadvantaged area, I can and do endorse all the facts so forcibly expressed in Davies's articles.

Name and address supplied

Nick Davies's article (Chris Woodhead's world of phoney facts, 16 September) contains the odd silliness.

He states that Ofsted did not publish figures for primary inspections five years ago. He is wrong. My first annual report, in 1993–94, stated that 30% of lessons in Key Stage 2 were unsatisfactory. This figure was not 'invented': it reflects the substantial number of primary inspections undertaken that year. He argues that on my own admission comparisons are impossible. The point, of course, is that changes to inspection methodology make precise comparisons year-on-year impossible. This in no way invalidates the broad comparisons between quality of teaching observed today and five years ago.

Our Class Size report analysed the quality of teaching and learning in schools in similar socio-economic circumstances. Ofsted's data shows that, in infant classes, smaller numbers of pupils in the class are associated with higher quality teaching and learning irrespective of the affluence or poverty of the community the school serves. For older children, aged eight to eleven years, there is no such association and class size appears to be a neutral factor.

I am not sure where Nick Davies found his inspectors queuing up to complain about a shortage of hard data. We give inspectors a very substantial amount of hard data in the Pre-inspection Context and School Indicators. Perhaps these were the same inspectors who said that a percentage of unsatisfactory lessons does not equate to a percentage of incompetent teachers. We have never said they do. We had a firm basis for our earlier estimate and we now have strong, factual evidence to confirm the statistics we quoted.

I am accused of having no data to support the claim that whole-class teaching generates better results. On the contrary, our recent publication, *Primary Education – A Review of Primary Schools in England 1994–98*, based on a massive amount of inspection evidence, from Section 10 reports and

HMI surveys, states that the factor that makes the most difference to the improvement of teaching methods is direct whole-class teaching.

Nick Davies might object to my 'acidic essay', but he cannot stand up the charge that we 'really don't know'. There has never been so much performance information as is now available in education. And the improvement in teaching I have identified is fully consistent with the sharp rise in standards identified both through inspection and in Key Stage test results.

Chris Woodhead
Chief Inspector of Schools

Put together Chris Woodhead's reply (Letters, September 18) to Nick Davies, and the quotation from him which Davies used, and we recognise the miasma of statistical ignorance and sloppy language which is characteristic of him.

He misquotes Davies's objection, which is that the comparisons with figures from five years later are not impossible but 'invalid'. 'Impossible' is Woodhead's own word. But he uses it of 'precise comparisons' only, not 'broad comparisons'. He fails to see the difference between imprecise and invalid, which is fundamental in statistics. A comparison can be imprecise yet valid, as Woodhead does indeed recognise. But if a comparison is invalid, then not even an imprecise judgment is legitimate. (For instance, smallish inaccuracies in results can make a decline look like an improvement.)

And after all it is Woodhead in the quotation who implicitly impugns not just precision but validity. He describes changes in both methods and standards used by inspectors as 'significant'. What does significant mean, if not that straight comparison is invalid? (Changing the number of grades used is a clear example here – significant because it impugns validity.) If comparison is still valid, then the changes are surely minor or trivial, not significant. In this quotation, Woodhead lacks the conceptual grasp to understand his own words. It's against that kind of failure that his further insistences to have 'substantial . . . hard data', 'a firm basis' for an estimate and 'strong, factual evidence:

must be understood and doubted. For literally, he doesn't seem to know the meanings of the words used to analyse and evaluate arguments.
Nigel Blake
Byfleet, Surrey

When Kenneth Baker was Secretary of State for Education and imposing savage cuts on school budgets, I attended a meeting for parents at my daughter's comprehensive, Camden School for Girls. The head teacher announced to a stunned audience that the head of classics was leaving the school and that Latin and Greek would not be taught in future. The gifted teacher would be taking over the classics department at Roedean. Kenneth Baker's daughters were educated at Roedean: no wonder he can afford to carry on laughing.
Caroline Compton
London

TWO

MONEY

MONEY MATTERS:
A TALE OF TWO SCHOOLS

6 MARCH, 2000

IT IS SPEECH day at Roedean College. The string orchestra plays Mozart's Divertimento in D as the parents gather in the Centenary Hall. They have come to hear the Chairman of Council report on the state of the school, to join the applause for the retiring staff and to watch the three head girls deliver their review of the year, but most of all, these mothers and fathers have come to salute the achievements of their children.

The head teacher, Patricia Metham, calls the girls up one by one, announcing their awards and their prizes and their exam results. 'Irina Allport, eight and a half passes at GCSE . . . Leonara Bowen, nine and a half passes . . . Angelica Chan, eleven passes.' The applause drenches the hall. Mrs Metham tells the parents that the school's results are the best in Sussex and place Roedean high in the first division of league tables. And the future? 'For those at Roedean,' Mrs Metham declares, 'it need hold no terrors.'

Down the grassy hill, on the far side of the Roedean playing fields, on this October Saturday, it is just another morning on the Whitehawk estate – some lads belting a football around East Brighton Park, someone hosing down a car, dogs sniffing at the dustbins. Whitehawk is a sprawl of terraced red-brick houses, home to something like 11,000 people, most of them white, many of them out of work. Whitehawk is the poorest estate in Brighton, and one of the poorest 10% in the whole country. It is the kind of place where almost everyone has suffered a crime and almost no one bothers to report it any more.

While Patricia Metham is celebrating the success of her pupils, another head teacher is having a very different experience. Libby Coleman spent three long years as the head teacher of Stanley Deason Comprehensive School on the Whitehawk estate, and now she sits at home, less than a mile away, staring out at the scruffy grey sea, looking back over those years which began with so much hope when she had no idea – really, none at all – that by the time she left, her career as a head, her health and the school would all be in ruins.

This is the story of two women. In many ways, they are quite separate – the secure and confident head of the famous old private school where almost every pupil scores at least five top grades at GCSE, and the rueful and defeated head of the state school, where only a tenth of the children could make the same mark. Just as Roedean turns in the best results in Sussex, so Whitehawk has made its mark with the very worst. The two women have never met. Their careers have been quite different. The narrow strip of Downland between Roedean and Whitehawk marks the most notorious division in British society. And yet, for all this separation, the two women have this in common, that after several decades in teaching, they know what makes schools tick.

A few weeks before Roedean's speech day, the Prime Minister, Tony Blair, appeared on *Channel 4 News* and talked about this same division. He made clear to Jon Snow how passionately he wants state schools to match the results of their counterparts in the private sector. You can see why. There are only 550,000 children in private schools in this country. They count for a mere 7% of the pupil population and yet they provide more than 20% of those who make it to university and nearly 50% of those who go to Oxford or Cambridge. In 1999 the *Financial Times* survey of A-level results revealed that all but thirteen of the top 100 schools were in the private sector. In the private schools, 80% of pupils pass five or more GCSEs at grades A to C; in the state schools, only 43% reach the same standard.

And why is this happening? In government circles, the answer has been agreed for years: teachers in state schools fail to do their job properly. The analysis is alarming: over a period of thirty years, beginning in the 1960s, the quest for excellence was undermined by an obsession with equality; student teachers were injected with a theory of child-centred learning which poisoned the heart of pedagogy, allowing the pupil to dictate the pace and direction of teaching; discipline and effort were banned from classrooms where no child might now be accused of failure; whole-class instruction gave way to groups of children ambling along at their own sweet speed; criticism was replaced by endless consolation, achievement was subverted by a poverty of expectation, aspiration was defeated by a relentless levelling down; the grammar schools were lost in a comprehensive fudge, all in the cause of social engineering. By contrast, on this view, the private schools were safely inoculated from this progressive disease by their traditions of competitive achievement, with the result, quite simply, that teachers in private schools now do the job better.

This perspective was born on the right as a rebuttal to the comprehensive movement. It was expressed with special clarity, for example, by the former Tory education minister George Walden, in his book, *We Should Know Better*:

The idea that every child can advance at his or her pace by informal, non-competitive techniques that favour spontaneity over effort is a beautiful dream which, lodged in impressionable minds and given scientific status, becomes unconscious dogma. In reality, it leads to over-stressed teachers, low aspirations for the gifted and un-gifted alike, bored or disaffected pupils, and an enormous waste of time and money. The contrast with the private sector needs little emphasis.

Right-wing journalists pursued the same critique with passion and found that, in opposition, Tony Blair's Labour Party had joined their crusade. In January 1996, *Sunday Times* columnist Melanie Phillips celebrated: 'They're now against bad teaching, fashionable education fallacies and failing schools. Terrific.' A year into the Blair government, a *Sunday Telegraph* columnist, Minette Marin, endorsed David

Blunkett's policies as the key to injecting the technique of private schools into the ailing world of their state counterparts: 'If teachers, teacher-trainers and professors of education all had a change of heart and decided to follow the example of the private schools and the old grammar schools, and to teach accordingly, that would not cost very much. All they would have to do would be to follow willingly the government's various plans for reform.'

It is now close to the heart of New Labour's approach to education, to see private schools not as an enemy to be abolished, but as a partner to be emulated – as 'a benchmark of best practice'. In the three months before Roedean's speech day, both the head of Ofsted, Chris Woodhead, and the Minister for School Standards, Estelle Morris, spoke at conferences of private head teachers, stressing their admiration for their work as a template for state school teachers. Since May 1997, the government has invested £1.6 million in bridge-building schemes to allow state school pupils to enjoy the technique of private school teaching.

It is explicit in this analysis that the strength of private schools is not to be explained by their intake of highly motivated children from affluent families, compared with the deprived and demotivated children in some state schools – 'poverty is no excuse' in the government's words. Nor is it to be explained by the extra resources or smaller class sizes in private schools, as Chris Woodhead has explained repeatedly, pointing instead to 'a toxic mix of educational beliefs and mismanagement' as the real problem. As the Department for Education recently told the *Guardian*: 'The quality of teaching is the main thing.'

Libby Coleman was full of hope when she first arrived at Whitehawk. It was January 1995. She had already been a head for ten years, first in Northampton and then in Barnet, she had done well – Ofsted had given her a report full of praise – and yet she wanted something different. In both her schools, she had seen deprived children struggling to make the grade and she believed passionately that she could help them, that poverty was no reason for failure. She was excited by all the new ideas which were bubbling out of the political world – literacy hours, numeracy hours, mentors, beacon schools – and so she had decided to move to a school that was really struggling with deprivation and to try to use these ideas to turn it around. It was an unusual thing to do, but she liked to be unconventional, to listen to her instincts before she listened to the rules. For her, it was a kind of crusade.

The Stanley Deason School in Whitehawk was certainly struggling with poverty. As soon as she arrived, Libby Coleman was struck by two things: some 45% of the children were poor enough to claim free school meals, nearly four times the national average (which is 12%); and almost all of them were white. There were no aspiring immigrants here, pushing their children to succeed. These were second- and third-generation long-term unemployed. By the time the children reached Stanley Deason, many had already fallen way behind. Among the Year Seven children when she arrived, she found only 10% of them had a reading age of eleven. And the attendance was terrible. On average, each morning, only 72% were turning up – more than a quarter of them simply never came through the door. By the afternoon, even more had faded away. And those who stayed often failed to go to the right classroom. Libby Coleman was undaunted. She could do it, she was sure.

As the weeks passed, she found the kids had a kind of wildness in them. There were children who reeked of lighter fluid: they had soaked their shirts in the stuff and hooked them up over their faces to suck in the flames. A thirteen-year-old boy had started working as a prostitute down on Duke's Mound on the Brighton waterfront: as far as Libby Coleman could find out, he had originally been seduced by his stepfather, who had then tried to cash in by taking the lad over to Amsterdam to sell him in the brothels there. Then she was dealing with this lovely, bright girl who certainly had the intelligence to reach the top level in her SATs, but she wouldn't speak. Not a sound. Libby Coleman had come across it before – an elective mute, often a sign of abuse. But when she asked about it, she was told there was hardly any point in pursuing it: there was so much sexual abuse of

67

children on Whitehawk that unless you had real evidence, no one was going to try and prove it.

In Whitehawk, she learned, the apparently simple could rapidly become bizarre and frightening. She was asked to find a place for a fourteen-year-old boy who had been expelled from another school. It should have been all right. As soon as she met him, she could see he had good in him, but within days, the boy was abducted from the estate by three men who drove him to some woods and took it in turns to rape him. She had the boy and his mother in afterwards to talk about it, but the mother was incoherent with tears and the boy attacked her. There was nothing she could do. He ended up in a locked ward.

Or there was a boy who was playing truant, which should have been fairly straightforward, but then it turned out that his mother had witnessed a gang of youths ram-raiding a local store and had then made the simple error of making a statement to the police. Now the thieves were threatening to kill her unless she withdrew her evidence, and the police were putting pressure on her not to back down, and so the lad was staying off school to try to protect her.

The parents were as troubled as the children. One day she held an open day for new parents, but a group of them turned on a young mother who had been a pupil there with them years ago and started taunting her, simply bullying her like beasts, just as they had done as children. The mother was so filled with childlike terror that she fled into Libby's office, where she quaked with fear and told her story and finally relieved her anxiety by vomiting across Libby's desk. Some parents disappeared, like the woman who had run off to London with her pimp, leaving her boy with his blind grandmother. Some cracked and ended up weeping in her arms in the middle of her room.

Still, this was why she had come here, to help kids who were in this kind of trouble. She was sure she would be all right. If there was nevertheless a problem that worried her, it was in the staff room. From the very first day, she had been warned she was in trouble. The vice-chair of the governors, a man called Robert Metcalfe, universally known as 'Met', was apparently dead set against her. He had once been a teacher in the school and risen to be deputy head and, even though he was retired, he seemed to look upon the place as his personal fiefdom. When the governors were looking for a new head, he had evidently backed another candidate and lost. Now, he was telling anyone who would listen that this Coleman woman was no bloody good – she was the kind who didn't understand that what kids really needed was a firm hand. Libby Coleman was warned that Met had several good friends in the staff room who were already sowing the seeds of dissent; they were telling everyone she would be out in less than six months.

Patricia Metham's study is a peaceful place. There is a group of wicker chairs with coloured cushions in front of the fireplace, a Persian rug on the carpet, a collection of sculpted hands on the chest by the wall, a computer, a printer, a teddy bear, a neat and tidy desk and, most of all, a picture window gazing down across the playing fields to the wide open sea. Mrs Metham is intelligent, forceful and very clear in her thinking.

First of all, she is clear that Roedean is not the school of familiar cliché, all fresh air and hockey sticks. It is a place of academic excellence but more than that, she says, it is a place of breadth, which prizes drama and dance and sport and music; and more even than that, she wants it to be a place for free thinkers. She was rather proud to find one of her old girls leading a rent strike at Oxford in 1999. 'Intelligent independence' is her mantra. It may be for this reason that although she knows very well what government ministers and conservative journalists say about private schools like hers, she does not agree with them. Not at all.

Teaching technique comes into their success, but her expectation has almost nothing in common with the government's analysis. It is built, first of all, on a simple foundation – the intake of children. 'Those schools that dominate the league tables choose to be and can afford to be highly selective.' Every pupil who wants to enter Roedean sits an exam. There are some schools which set tougher papers, but the Roedean paper is quite tough enough to ensure that those eleven-year-olds who pass and who enter the school are among the brightest and the best.

Roedean routinely puts its newly selected Year Seven pupils through Cognitive Ability Tests. Last year, not a single child was below the national average for non-verbal or quantitative skills. Most were clearly above average. Some were rated 'very high'. And all of them could read. Mrs Metham goes further. It is not just that these children have their academic engines already running when they reach the school, but they also tend to be from homes which have impressed on them the need to take education seriously: 'On the whole, we have highly motivated pupils and highly motivated parents.' On most days, she will see at least one set of parents who are interested in the school. The contrast with the state sector needs little emphasis.

This is the most important part of the story – the intake of able children from supportive families – but it is by no means the end of the explanation. In 1997 the London School of Economics produced a revealing study in which they compared the educational achievements of students who went to private schools on the old Assisted Place Scheme with the achievements of those who had been offered an assisted place but turned it down and opted to stay in the state sector. The LSE checked the verbal and non-verbal reasoning scores of their two groups and confirmed that the two sets of students were very similar in their ability. And yet, by the time they came to take their A levels, the group who had opted for the private schools had clearly pulled ahead. First, they had sat more exams and, second, they had gained better results than those who had stayed in the state schools. Translated into A-level grades, the children who went through the private schools were achieving between one and a half and three grades higher than their equivalents who had stayed in the state sector – the difference, for example, between three A grades and three B grades. The intake of children is clearly important but equally clearly, as a mass of educational research has shown, schools can make some difference. In the first place, the successful private schools are selecting talent. But they are also developing it.

On the Whitehawk estate, life at Stanley Deason was sometimes like being inside a threshing machine as one incident crashed down on the tail of another. One moment, there was a senior woman teacher in tears because an eleven-year-old boy had spat at one of the girls and reacted to being ticked off by turning round and farting in the teacher's face. The next, there was a neighbouring school on the phone complaining that two Whitehawk girls had been down there with razor knives, trying to cut up a girl who had been flirting with one of their boyfriends. A boy kicked out a water pipe and flooded the library below. Someone set a fire in the toilets. And then Ofsted said they wanted to come and inspect the place.

Still Libby Coleman knew what she wanted. She wasn't so sure whether she could pay for it. Early on, she had discovered to her horror that the school roll was carrying 'ghost children' – at least thirty kids who were enrolled in the school, whose names were being ticked off on class registers, who were being funded by the local education authority, and who were essentially fictitious. Either they had been at the school but left long ago or else, so far as she could tell, they had never existed in the first place. She called her union. It was fraud, they said, and she could go to prison. 'Prison?' she said. 'I don't do going to prison.' So she called the LEA and told them all about it. The ghosts were exorcised from the roll and the school lost something like £40,000 out of its annual budget.

At first, Libby Coleman thought she could live with the loss. Miraculously, the school had managed to store up £80,000 in its reserves and so there was a cushion. Except that there wasn't. The money was nowhere to be found. She called in two sets of auditors in search of the cash, but it was not there: £80,000 had simply gone missing.

She wanted more teachers. There was no chance of that; the whole LEA was being told to expect a cut across the board. She wanted to buy a computer program called Success Maker.

71

The Year Seven children could work with it on their own, it would stretch each child to an appropriate level and free up teachers. But there was no money for that. In fact, there was no money for computers generally, and the only ones they had were too old to take any software that used Windows. She tried to tackle the truants: calling the parents as soon as the child was missing, following up in writing, and posting the attendance figures on the noticeboard. She thought it would help to give prizes for the class with the best attendance and for three pupils who most improved their attendance. She knew there was no money for that, so she paid for the prizes herself.

The whole school was struggling to drag itself forward, and she could see the stress pumping through her staff. There were teachers who simply lost it and sobbed or climbed up on a chair and started yelling uncontrollably at the children. She saw one teacher screaming at a boy: 'You're useless, you're completely worthless.' Libby had not known what was most upsetting – to see a teacher reduced to such hysteria or to see a child's self-respect so battered. In any case, she had gone off to the toilets to be sick.

There were so many staff off ill. An English teacher had died and everyone said it was stress. Another, who was known as Shergar, had simply disappeared. There were several who developed very serious illnesses – cancer of the kidney, cancer of the colon. One of the art teachers had a breakdown, the head of maths left in tears, the new science teacher cracked up and took six months off. Only the most talented teachers could thrive against these odds. A few did – really great teachers. There were others who limped along like walking wounded – with no kind of help or support from anyone in the school or the LEA – constantly calling in sick, constantly forcing the school to hire supply teachers who cost yet more money and, with the best will in the world, could not handle a class full of strangers. And then there were those who, Libby Coleman believed, should never have come near a classroom in their lives, teachers who treated children with contempt, who were glad when they truanted because it made life easier, and who were quite happy to manhandle them when it suited them.

She wanted to get rid of these really bad ones, but she couldn't. It was not just that the law involved a twelve-month obstacle course, policed at every stage by unions who would jump on the tiniest procedural fault, but, worse than that, she would need the support of the governors and most of the really bad teachers were also allies of 'Met' Metcalfe, the vice-chair of governors, who was now making no secret of his desire to oust her. Soon she was fighting a cold war against this group of teachers who treated her openly with contempt. From time to time she would discipline a teacher for man-handling a student and there would be a storm of whispers in the staff room. Teachers who had no time for Met and his gang of troublemakers began to worry that Libby Coleman was creating a culture where children were encouraged to dish dirt on teachers, whether it was true or not. Some began to say it was her fault they were suffering such stress, because she was so quick to criticise, winding people up to breaking point. The cold war began to spread.

Several times, she went to her desk to find that someone had been looking through her papers. She began to take sensitive work home. As she identified more problems, she found her working day stretching, from eight in the morning until late at night, spilling all over the weekend, trying to motivate the students, trying to energise the parents, trying to activate the staff, firing off ideas – teaching parents how to help their children revise, cadging old computers off local firms, calming disruptive kids in exams by having their parents sit with them. But every solution seemed to spawn another problem. (There were teachers who were furious with her when she succeeded in steering the most unruly pupils back into their classrooms.) Soon, the tide of tension was starting to reach her too.

She had this lurking feeling of sickness. She found she was grinding her front teeth almost all the time, she realised that her neck and shoulders were constantly tight, in fact the tension ran all the way up around her skull and into her forehead, her head ached, she was smoking more and more – up to thirty a day now – and at night she was having trouble sleeping. Sometimes, in the evening, she would drink whisky to force the tiredness upon her, but then she would wake in the small hours and wander around the house, smoking and squeezing her hands. She realised just how bad she was becoming after an incident when a girl refused to come to school because she had been gang-raped by several boys, some of them from her own class. The police seemed unable to act, Libby really could not see a solution in the classroom, and so the girl left. Which was tough. But what really shocked her was when she realised that her sadness for the girl had been quickly invaded by quite a different feeling – a curse that this meant she would lose the couple of thousand pounds funding that went with her. She was getting chest pains, too. But there was no time to worry about any of that. Ofsted were on the way.

By the time they arrived, in May 1996, she had been running the school for fifteen months. Things had improved a little, but not enough. The Ofsted team did a good job. The measure of that was that they told Libby Coleman what she already knew: not enough children were coming to school; too many children were failing exams; the school was in deficit and was going to have to make cuts to stay alive; and 'the new head teacher is trying to bring about improvements but needs support to do so'. Privately, one of them told her that they had never come across such treachery from colleagues.

The Ofsted team offered her their own version of support, but it was not a kind she welcomed. They suggested the school should be put into 'special measures', and said it would help: the LEA would have to give more support, she could get a better budget, the staff would have to work together to keep the school open. But Libby Coleman was worried. She knew special measures could be a poisoned chalice – the school would be branded a failure, the brand would be displayed for all to see and, in the absence of miracles, the few remaining middle-class families would run, taking precious money with them. If she was really unlucky, the best staff would start running too. And this was all the help that was on offer.

She went home, too exhausted to think. It was half-term

and she truly believed she was dying. She could not speak, she could only shuffle, and she stayed cocooned in fatigue, wondering whether she might be rescued by death, until the half-term week ended and she had go to back. In the car, with her mind pumping, she felt one side of her body go dead. She looked in the rear-view mirror and saw her face was bloodless, her lips were grey. She managed to drive to the hospital, where they tested her and told her there was nothing wrong, at least not physically.

Patricia Metham is proud to show you her school: the chapel with the neo-classical ceiling and the Byzantine marble; through the quiet cloisters to the renaissance garden; into the language labs (French, German, Spanish, Italian, Mandarin Chinese, and English as a foreign language for pupils from abroad); the science labs; and then the network of libraries containing 20,000 books as well as a collection of videos and CDs and twenty-five computers linked to the Internet. Here is the Roedean Theatre, with 350 seats; the dance studio – 'one of the best in the country' – used for jazz as well as ballet; the art studio, the design technology suite, where some of the sixth-form girls have been stripping down an old Austin; the six indoor netball courts, two indoor cricket nets, one indoor hockey pitch, the fitness gym and full-sized indoor pool.

It is no secret why a private school may do more for its children than a state school. Mrs Metham might be forgiven if she chose to agree with the government that it is simply because she and her staff know more about teaching, but her answer is less self-serving. Money. 'If the government want state schools to offer what we offer, they are going to have to spend on each child something much closer to the fees that our parents pay. At the moment, there is such an enormous gap.' Roedean is paid £10,260 a year for a day girl, roughly five times the amount which a school like Whitehawk is given per pupil.

Money shows not only in physical resources but also right at the heart of the school's business, where the teacher meets the child. It is very simple: 'We can do better than a state school with equivalent ability range because of our class sizes.' The biggest classes in Roedean may have as many as twenty girls, usually a highly motivated group of the same standard, but for those who are not so confident or who are approaching big exams, classes are much smaller, sometimes as small as three. The pupil:staff ratio across the whole of Roedean is only 8:1. For Patricia Metham, this is central: 'The point is that we can really match our approach to teaching to what experience tells us works.'

And, although she and her staff may work hard, they are not collapsing under stress and illness. She insists that 'I am a bossy and interfering woman and I like to get involved', but she does not drown. From the calm of her study, she watches the whole school work: staff come to see her about projects; prospective parents come to be shown around the school; there's a problem with the catering or a homesick girl; the bursar may come in to talk about the budget; she writes letters, she sees pupils. Then she goes home, to a listed building in the style of William Morris in the centre of the school grounds.

If Patricia Metham is right – that this combination of a bright intake and adequate resources is the real foundation of her school's success – nevertheless, there is more to her account. There is yet a third factor which finally defines the division between these two educational worlds.

Libby Coleman knew her school was one step away from closure. She turned to the authorities for help, but the Department of Education took five months just to authorise her action plan. The local education authority was being broken up, and the staff were too busy reapplying for their jobs to look out for her. Ofsted were supposed to come back each term but chose to disappear for a year. She was alone. Worse, just as she had feared, the announcement of special measures was driving some families away from the school; that meant the budget was being cut and the governors were looking for redundancies. The staff room was a snakepit of dissent and depression. As a direct result of the special measures, every teacher's job was now threatened; everyone knew they were being watched and judged; every day now, at least half-a-dozen teachers would call in sick. Met's allies were constantly whispering against her – the person whose judgement would decide their future – and she knew a lot of the others were blaming her for failing to protect them, for criticising their own failure, for raising their hopes in the first place.

She poured out ideas: catch-up lessons for poor attenders, spot-checks on attendance, a welfare officer for the lower school, work experience for older children, CCTV to stop vandals, a working party on staff absence, mentors for Year Ten pupils, teachers to visit other schools, new homework programmes, shorter lessons, more lessons. But she was trapped by lack of funds and lack of support and by the special measures themselves. The staff were demanding that some of the most difficult children be excluded, but the rules of special measures forbade it. For her part, Libby had already identified the staff who ought to go, but the fact was that she could not get rid of them because no good teacher was going to replace them, not if it meant coming to a school in special measures. The students started to roam wild in the corridors; she set patrols of teachers with bleepers and walkie-talkies to hold the line against chaos. She stopped eating and started smoking like a gangster. Most days, she was riddled with stress.

Eventually, in mid-1997, more than a year after Ofsted's visit, HM inspectors came back and said things were improving, and the new Brighton and Hove authority came up with some money for a senior teacher and for the Success Maker software. They refused to fund a summer school for poor readers but she scraped a grant from a crime charity. That September, the school was relaunched with a new name – Marina High – and a new uniform and it became the first secondary school in the country to introduce a literacy hour. Metcalfe's term on the governing body came to an end. She began to think things might be all right.

However, she soon began to see that there were too many holes in the boat. The students had had a riotous summer, burning out half-a-dozen police cars on the estate. The police said some of the children were working for a new drugs syndicate who had moved down from Glasgow. The few new teachers she had hired were drowning in disorder in the classroom. One of them walked out for good. She decided to bring in a counsellor to help with some of the wilder children.

He arrived to find workmen removing her study door (someone had smashed a fist through it), and Libby tried to explain that she had lost her sixth girl that year, pregnant; that a seventeen-year-old former student had just been murdered on the rubbish tip next to the school; that the brother of one student had just been accused of helping to murder the father of another; that a boy had been run down on the crossing outside the school; that she herself had just had her purse stolen by a Year Eight girl who had evidently given it to her older sister, who was a prostitute, and that this older sister had used her credit cards, and so the police had traced her to a flat where they had found her dead from a heroin overdose along with her boyfriend, and so now the Year Eight girl had been taken into care and it was her friends who were upset and needed extra counselling. The counsellor said he would have to see what he could do. The caretaker put on a new door.

In November, HM inspectors came back, saw a rotten collection of lessons, and narrowly escaped disaster when someone chucked firecrackers at them in a crowded corridor at breaktime. In December, the LEA warned her the school would close if there was not a dramatic change. She went home for Christmas in a fog of defeat. She had had four sessions with a psychiatrist to try to release her stress, but now she carried so much tension in her shoulders and neck that her jaw locked tight and she lost the ability to speak. At night she wept and thought of herself as a sin-eater, absorbing all of the anger and blame of everyone from her staff to the Secretary of State. She lay in bed, drenched in sweat, and then walked around the house in the dark, although now she was too tired to wake and did the walking in her sleep.

Within weeks of the new term, she knew she was hurtling to disaster. In a single week, children made two serious allegations of assault against staff. She followed the correct procedure and suspended both teachers while she investigated. The staff room went berserk, but when she investigated and reported that both allegations were groundless, the staff refused to be pacified and became even more irritated. And in the meantime the DFEE and the LEA and Ofsted and HM inspectors were all demanding results, and the more that Libby passed on the pressure to the staff, the more they hated her. Some of them wrote an anonymous letter to the LEA saying the school was in chaos and Libby was mad; the former governor, 'Met' Metcalfe, phoned the LEA and demanded that they sack her.

In February 1998, the DFEE paid a lightning visit to the school and did not like what they saw. HM inspectors were due back. Shortly before they arrived, Libby Coleman went to the LEA and told them she could not go on, and they agreed to let her go with a decent package if she would agree to stay for the HMI visit. The inspectors came and shook their heads. They took Libby aside to tell her she had done her best and reported that the school was still failing. It was Libby Coleman's last day. She felt mad with fatigue and maybe with relief, almost speechless with lockjaw, crushed by defeat. She went for one last walk through the school, leaning on the arm of a visiting deputy head. A Year Eight girl saw her. 'Are you pissed, Miss?' she said. 'No, darling – just very tired.' The next day, she resigned. She was fifty-two and she would never teach again.

When she was talking to the parents at Roedean's speech day, Patricia Metham made a small joke at David Blunkett's expense and then warned her audience: 'It's not easy being a teacher these days. What other profession is so beset by "experts" who haven't ever done the job themselves and who wouldn't last five minutes in a real school? Having in the distant past been a pupil is felt by too many to be qualification enough to dictate terms to those who are trained and experienced professionals.' But nobody dictates terms to the teachers in Roedean. They are not answerable to David Blunkett or his department or the LEA or Ofsted. They are not bound by the national curriculum or SATs tests or special measures or any of the other proliferating superstructure of supervision which has settled over the state schools. And that is the third factor in Roedean's success – freedom to teach as they think best.

Mrs Metham cites, as an example, the electric car project. Her head of physics decided that Year Nine would learn a lot from designing and building an electric car, to be entered into a competition at Goodwood racecourse, and so he rewrote the whole physics course for them. Mrs Metham said: 'We didn't have to check whether it fitted with Attainment Target A or whether the ticks would be in the right boxes. Being independent, we can choose how best to excite and inform our pupils – free from bureaucratic constraints. That is what being a professional is all about. I would find it very hard to be a head in the maintained sector.

'The difficulty is that all teachers in the maintained sector have been constrained by the same rather rigid bureaucracy and requirements. If you talk to people who have had a really good educational experience, nine times out of ten they will tell you about the charismatic teacher who stimulated an interest in a subject, an idiosyncratic person who knew enough about pacing and matching, understanding what was required. At independent schools, teachers are highly accountable, to the head teacher and to the parents, but how they get their results and what they do in the classroom or in a department, the judgement is left to them.'

Libby Coleman is better now. She has recovered her health and found new work as a consultant. The school on the Whitehawk estate never recovered and finally closed, eight months after her departure. All of the teachers lost their jobs. Looking now at the yawning gap between her school and Roedean, just across the fields, Libby Coleman finds a kind of unity with her counterpart. The two head teachers with their very separate experience can see the same three factors at work in their success and in their failure: the intake of motivated children; the provision of resources; the freedom to be professional. The stars of the private sector have all three. The perceived failures of the state sector work with none of them. In each case, the state sector has suffered from government policy: from the Tory reforms of the late 1980s which polarised the intake of children in state schools, concentrating the least motivated into struggling schools like Whitehawk; from the historic underfunding of British state education, which has been reversed by New Labour only in rhetoric; and from the enormity of the current interference by the DFEE and its agents with their highly politicised analysis. The great irony here is that the DFEE are trying to emulate private schools by adopting a superstructure of reforms which, almost without exception, is regarded with fear and contempt by the private schools themselves. Indeed, they cite their exemption from this superstructure as a key factor in their success.

In the most superficial sense, the analysis of the government and the conservative journalists is right: the quality of teaching is worse in some state schools, and so is the quality of learning. But this is not because they use different techniques or rely on different theories. Indeed, almost without exception, teachers in the state sector have been trained at the same college in the same techniques and with the same ideology as their private counterparts. Whitehawk had no special involvement with progressive teaching. On the contrary, its most troublesome teachers were a cynical breed of authoritarians. Roedean has no special attachment to traditional methods, such as the whole-class teaching which is embraced with such passion by Chris Woodhead and his followers. Patricia Metham says there are times when classes should be taught as a whole and others when they should be taught in small groups. 'Differentiation is the key,' she says. She herself learned her teaching in the state sector.

There is almost no connection at all between reality and the easy consensus of distant journalists and politicians. The real division, it transpires, is not between the teachers of the two different sectors, but between the practitioners, on the one side, and the politicians and the pundits on the other. The great advantage of the current official consensus is that it allows the politicians to deny all responsibilities for failure which is, on their account, entirely the fault of teachers, many of whom now collapse in stress and lose their jobs as a result.

The great irony is that David Blunkett sits in his office, lost in admiration for the success of the private sector, entirely failing to understand that the key to that success is his own absence from their schools.

THE £19 BILLION LIE – HOW MR BLUNKETT FIDDLED THE FIGURES

7 MARCH 2000

THERE ARE MANY mysteries in David Blunkett's Department for Education, but the greatest of them all is this: where has all the money gone?

On 14 July 1998, Mr Blunkett announced a spending bonanza for schools. 'The government is providing an additional £19 billion for education over the three years from 1999 to 2002,' he said. This was a very great deal of extra money. The annual budget for the entire educational establishment in the whole of the United Kingdom in 1998 was only £38.3 billion.

Mr Blunkett declared that this was 'an historic day for education and for the country' and 'the fulfilment of our pledge that education would be our number one priority'. These resources, he explained, would transform standards in the education service, boost literacy and numeracy for those under eleven, cut truancy and exclusion by a third, and give half a million more people access to higher and further education. More than that, he went on to pledge that this extra £19 billion would 'give everyone in our society the opportunity to realise their full potential'.

Ever since then, Mr Blunkett has pointed repeatedly to this extra £19 billion as the touchstone of New Labour's commitment to Britain's schools. When he wrote for the *Guardian* in reply to the first part of this series, for example, he said: 'Of course, our education policy is backed by substantial extra resources. The extra £19bn over three years is real.'

Eighteen months after the announcement, there is little sign of this torrent of extra resources sweeping through our schools and colleges. On the contrary, we have found that the education budget is so tight that in November 1999 Mr Blunkett's officials were forced to make emergency changes to keep local education authorities in the black. And when we conducted our own survey of local authorities, all but one of them reported that they had schools whose budgets were locked into deficit. Leeds, for example, said that sixty-eight of its 299 schools are in deficit; Somerset had thirty-two schools in the red, with a total deficit of £776,000; Northumbria had thirty-four; Staffordshire had twenty-nine; Rotherham had thirty-nine.

So where is the £19 billion? Maybe it is already in the schools and we have simply failed to observe it. Maybe it is on its way down the pipeline and will arrive any week now. Or maybe the truth is that there never was an additional £19 billion for education. Maybe Mr Blunkett's £19 billion is largely composed of magical money, billions which have been conjured out of thin air by trickery – double counting, treble counting, several different book-keeping manoeuvres and a steady stream of fundamentally misleading public statements. Watch closely and you can see the conjuror at work. The first trick is the biggest.

Ever since the birth of inflation, government departments have been increasing their spending each year. When David Blunkett made his grand announcement on 14 July 1998, he was reporting the results for education of Gordon Brown's Comprehensive Spending Review (CSR), which had laid down a budget for every Whitehall department for each of the final three years of the Parliament. The existing budget for UK education, for 1998/9, was £38.3 billion. As a result of the CSR, Mr Blunkett was able to announce that this would rise, in 1999, by £3 billion; in 2000, by £3.5 billion; and finally, in 2001/2, by £3.2 billion. That was all he announced. But, of course that adds up to only £9.7 billion. Where was the rest of the £19 billion? The answer is that it does not exist. Contrary to Mr Blunkett's description of his £19 billion as 'real', nearly half of it is manufactured by a single book-keeping trick.

It works like this. You take the increase for the first year and you say: 'Well, if I pay this in the first year, it will become a permanent part of the budget, so I will still be paying it in subsequent years when I make further annual increases, so I should carry on counting it as an increase each year.' This is not the way that any British government has previously accounted for its budgets. Carl Emmerson of the Institute for Fiscal Studies says it is 'misleading'; David Heald, professor of accountancy at Aberdeen University and a special adviser to the Treasury Select Committee, says it is 'confusing' and that 'most people were astounded by it, there is no precedent for it'.

But, for Mr Blunkett, the result was simply excellent. In Year One he had a rise of £3 billion. In Year Two he had a rise of £3.5 billion, but he added in the £3 billion which he would still be paying from Year One and called it a rise of £6.5 billion. Then he came to Year Three, when he had a rise of £3.2 billion, but he added in the £6.5 billion which he had already committed to the budget in the first two years and called it a rise of £9.7 billion. Then he stood back and added the whole lot up – £3 billion plus £6.5 billion plus £9.7 billion. A £19.2 billion bonanza.

In principle, there is nothing to stop the government pursuing this creative arithmetic for every subsequent year. For 2002, for example, Mr Blunkett might announce the lowest increase in education spending for years – say a meagre £2 billion. But by then he would be able to count his 1999 money four times, his 2000 money three times, his 2001 money twice. And so his meagre £2 billion would become a super soaraway mega-rise of £30.9 billion. If he is still running education at the end of a second Labour Parliament, Mr Blunkett will be in a position to announce annual rises which will wipe out the debt of whole continents.

This analysis cannot be news to Mr Blunkett or, indeed, to the Chancellor of the Exchequer, Gordon Brown, whose officials dreamed it up, for this is not the *Guardian*'s discovery. The wizardry in the arithmetic was spotted within two weeks of the original announcement by no less a source than the Treasury Select Committee. This committee of MPs interviewed all of the key people who had been involved in delivering the Comprehensive Spending Review, including Gordon Brown and his then chief secretary, Alistair Darling; they also took advice from three independent experts in public finance. Despite the fact that this committee is dominated by Labour MPs, they filed a highly critical report, dated 27 July 1998.

In the report – which received virtually no public attention at all – the MPs took one look at David Blunkett's £19 billion and saw straight through the figures. They came to two conclusions about this and about a comparable stunt with the health budget. First, in the most courteous terms, they told the government to stop playing with the numbers: 'We recommend that, for the sake of transparency, in future the government should refer to annual increases over the previous year, rather than a cumulative total.' Second, they noted how the media had 'faithfully reproduced' the misleading numbers and stated their own view: 'There is no cash bonanza of the type which newspaper headlines might suggest.'

The truth is that for his first two years in power, Mr Blunkett actually invested less in education than the Tories had been doing, and by the end of this Parliament, with all of his increases in place, he will still be only marginally ahead of the Tory level of spending – a level which he used to describe as 'miserable'. This was uncovered by researchers in the House of Commons library who reviewed the pattern of funding for education throughout the entire period from Margaret Thatcher's first day in power, in April 1979, to John Major's last, in May 1997, and worked out the average annual rise for the Tory years.

They projected that forward for the five years of this Parliament and compared the result with Mr Blunkett's budgets (even though, as we shall see, these figures are themselves questionable). They found that in his first year (looking at England alone) Mr Blunkett spent £324 million less than the projected Tory level. In his second year, he undershot them again, by £323 million. In the current year, 1999/2000, Labour have finally begun to nudge ahead of Tory spending levels, with an increase of £770 million; but even in the fifth year, with the maximum effect of their new budget, Labour will still be spending only £3 billion a year more on education in England than the Tories would have done if they had stayed in office and pursued their 'miserable' pattern – £38.8 billion compared to the £35.8 billion projected for the Tories. The additional £19 billion is nowhere to be seen.

One of the few MPs who have woken up to what has been happening is Phil Willis, the Lib Dem spokesman on education, who has been bombarding Mr Blunkett with parliamentary questions. 'The education bonanza is just an old-fashioned con-trick,' he said. 'Ministers have been evading my questions. When we asked about the delays, civil servants told my staff that I had tabled "the questions from hell". If Labour really had a record to be proud of, the truth would not hurt so much.'

Even though the Treasury Select Committee's alarm call passed almost entirely without notice in Parliament and Fleet Street (coverage consisted of part of one short story in the *Scotsman*), there can be no doubt that Mr Blunkett's officials and ministers know that their £19 billion claim was found to be bogus. This is not simply because the select committee report threatened to tear the guts out of their spending claims, but also because one of the Labour MPs who sat on the Treasury Committee and endorsed that report was Charles Clarke who, only twenty-four hours after publishing it, became David Blunkett's Minister for Schools. None of which has stopped the Secretary of State for Education, his officials and his ministers from continuing on every possible occasion to mislead the public and Parliament with the same phoney figure.

But this is not the end of the conjuring. Not even nearly. For example, not content with the magical conversion of £9.7 billion into £19 billion, Mr Blunkett and his ministers have indulged repeatedly in a second kind of trickery, in which they have recycled money through a sequence of different announcements, each time pretending that they are unveiling new spending when, in truth, they are simply delivering old money in new clothes. The distortion can be huge. Once again, if you watch closely, you can see the sleight-of-hand.

On 26 June 1997, the DFEE announced they would spend £100 million to fulfil Labour's pledge to cut the size of classes for infants. Five months later, on 17 November, the then Schools Minister, Stephen Byers, announced the release of £22 million to cut infant classes. But, in truth, this was part of the original £100 million which had already been announced. Eleven days later, Mr Byers announced the spending of £100 million to cut infant classes. It was the same money again. Two months after that, on 12 February 1998, Mr Blunkett himself stepped forward to announce the spending of £22 million on cutting infant classes. If anyone was beginning to become suspicious, they may have been reassured that Mr Blunkett explicitly stated that this was new money, referring to 'the £22 million of Standards Fund money that I am announcing today . . .' The truth, however, is that it was the same money all over again. The combined implication of the four statements was that the government were releasing £244 million; in fact, they had released only £100 million.

Sometimes, in the small print at the end of the statement, the department acknowledges the truth. Invariably, this does not make its way into press reports and invariably ministers do nothing to correct the misleading impression that is left. In this same way, the department has also recycled its PFI funding. A year after David Blunkett announced that schools would receive £1 billion of PFI credits, the department issued a statement which began: 'Schools will receive a £1 billion private finance boost, Schools minister Jacqui Smith announced today.' It was the same money. They have done it with the Sure Start scheme for pre-school children, with computer schemes for teachers, the national numeracy drive and computers for poor families. David Blunkett announced £575 million of capital support for local authorities and Voluntary Aided schools. Three weeks later: 'Schools minister Charles Clarke today announced allocations to Local Education Authorities and schools of £575 million . . .'

The distortion in some of the recycling is breath taking. On 25 November 1999, for example, Mr Blunkett found an extra £64 million for local education authorities and also saved schools some £90 million by allowing them to delay new contributions to teacher pensions. This net improvement of £154 million was announced by his department with the following words: 'An increase of £1.8 billion for local education authorities in England was announced by Education and Employment Secretary David Blunkett today.' Mr Blunkett had managed this huge leap by recycling £1.6 billion of funding which, so far from being 'announced today', had been revealed and repeatedly discussed for up to sixteen months.

The Press Release Trick has added layers of confusion to the original double and treble counting, but now, if we dispel Mr Blunkett's illusion that he is constantly announcing new money, we come back to his £19 billion; and if we also dispel the multiple counting, we can see that all he is really offering is an increase of £9.7 billion over the last three years of the Parliament. But no – he is not offering even that much.

For a start, he has taken no account of inflation in his figures. In real terms, according to the House of Commons library, in 1997/8 prices, Mr Blunkett is actually talking about an increase over these three years of £1.9 billion in 1999; £2.3 billion in 2000; and £1.9 billion in 2001/2. In other words, his £19 billion bonanza now shrinks to only £6.1 billion. Even that would be a substantial increase, particularly in comparison to the Tory years, but look more closely.

In order to work with the figures which are publicly available, we have to forget for a moment that Mr Blunkett has ignored inflation and go back to the three-year rise of £9.7 billion. Now, ask two questions: first, how much of this money is real and not simply the result of yet more book-keeping stunts; and, second, to the extent that it proves to be real, how much of it is additional funding and not simply the extra cash which is needed to keep pace with new demands – not just inflation but rising pupil numbers, new pension obligations and so on?

The conjuring is well concealed. While the DFEE insists on transparency from others, its own budget remains opaque. The department, for example, claims to have no information at all about £1.6 million of this money which is earmarked for education in Scotland, Wales and Northern Ireland. It simply disappears off the books. But we can still try to trace the lion's share of the rise, the supposed increase of £8.1 billion which Mr Blunkett says will bring such rewards to education in England from 1999 to 2002. The short story is that there is some extra money here, but the political claim easily overshoots the reality. Although the DFEE's lack of transparency makes it impossible finally to put a figure on the truth, it is clear that the real new benefit turns out to be substantially less than £8.1 billion. The money is to be paid out under three headings.

The first part of the £8.1 billion increase which Mr Blunkett claims to be spending in England is £1.2 billion for capital works – i.e. repairs and new buildings. In a way, this is a repeat of the Press Release Trick – real money dressed up in hyperbole.

The government's problem with the physical fabric of schools is immense. Estimates of the cost of repairing and replacing buildings which were neglected during the Tory years run as high as £20 billion. A 1995 survey found 600 primary schools still using outside toilets. John Lennon's old school in Liverpool still uses a temporary canteen that was erected during the last war. Engineers have advised Bradfield Comprehensive in Sheffield to put a wind gauge on top of their mobile classrooms so that they can evacuate the children before a storm takes the rotting roofs off.

This £1.2 billion is part of a £5.4 billion programme for capital works over the next three years which was announced by Mr Blunkett in November 1998. In its flourish of optimism, the announcement echoed his claims for the £19 billion: 'This investment could enable major repairs in thousands more schools . . . This substantial investment . . . transform our schools . . . a new beginning . . . regenerating local economies and boosting the surrounding communities.'

Anyone who heard this announcement would be forgiven for believing that the government was going to invest £5.4 billion in capital works for schools over the next three years. However, they would have been wrong. Schools ministers have since recycled the announcement, claiming explicitly that the government is investing this money. But they are not.

What the government is actually investing in school buildings over the three years is only some £1.735 billion: £1.085 billion from the New Deal for Schools, announced by Gordon Brown in his 1997 budget as part of his windfall tax; and a further estimated £0.65 billion in cash grants for voluntary-aided church schools and former grant-maintained schools. The rest of the £5.4 contains more magical money and a degree of exaggeration.

£0.8 billion has been conjured out of thin air. Contrary to being an investment by the government, this money will come from the hard-pressed local authorities – if it comes from anywhere. Contrary to being real cash, it turns out to be what the DFEE describes as a 'notional' contribution – a Whitehall estimate of money that the local authorities might be able to come up with by selling land and buildings or by diverting cash from the rest of their education budget or from other programmes. Or they might not. The figure is there; the bold announcement is made; only time will tell if the cash materialises. And none of it will come from the government.

The remaining £2.9 billion does at least represent a contribution from central government, but it is not cash. It consists of 'credit approvals' and 'PFI credits' – i.e. permission to borrow cash, either from the Public Works Board or from private finance partners. Under PFI, for example, the government are saying that for each of the three years, LEAs can take part in PFI projects worth £350 million. What the government is actually investing is nothing like that – in the ten months of this financial year, for example, they have spent only £6.28 million on PFI in schools.

The permission to borrow, supported by payments from Whitehall, is arguably a real asset to local authorities although these schemes – particularly the PFI ones – are far more complex than simple cash transactions. A group of Cardiff schools, for example, who are desperate for PFI funding for new buildings, have been turned down flat. Some schools and councillors are deeply suspicious of handing over ownership of their school buildings to private financiers.

Others have engaged in expensive and time-consuming presentations in an attempt to secure approval for PFI schemes. As with the notional LEA money, it is too soon to know how many of these credits will actually materialise. With only two months of the 1999/2000 financial year to run, schools had taken up only 53% of the PFI credits on offer for the year.

Most of this £5.4 billion programme of cash and borrowing sits outside the £19 billion scheme – it cannot be presented as new spending by the DFEE. Only a £1.2 billion slice fits. This consists of some cash, in grants for voluntary-aided church schools and former grant-maintained schools and also for higher and further education and special projects. But there is no new cash for mainstream LEA schools, only credit approvals. The bottom line, however, is that, despite the misleading hyperbole and despite the fact that there is not nearly as much real, new cash as the government has claimed, capital projects in schools and colleges are likely to receive from one source or another something close to the extra £1.2 billion which the government has quoted. The same cannot be said of the second heading of funding in the supposed increase of £8.1 billion.

This is an extra £3.6 billion for English local education authorities to spend over the last three years of the Parliament. This is the core of education funding: a school gets its entire annual budget from its local authority. But how much of it is real and new? Here Mr Blunkett is performing the political equivalent of cutting his lovely assistant in half with a saw. The trick is so old that the audience really ought to be able to see through it, and yet it's so good that it still fools them every time.

What Mr Blunkett announced was an increase in the education Standard Spending Assessment and, even if his audience don't understand, he knows that an SSA is not money at all but simply a Whitehall guideline to indicate the level of spending which the government says would be appropriate. The money is hidden away in the conjuror's other hand, under a heading called Total External Support (TES), which consists of Rate Support Grant and a central pool of business rates and various smaller grants, all of which are paid out to the local authorities through the Department of Environment. Don't look at the SSA. Look at the TES.

You have to look carefully here, because governments use a traditional but highly effective concealment. They announce SSA guidelines for each area of local authority work – not just education but social services and road maintenance and so on. But when it comes to providing the money in TES, they don't break it down. They simply announce a lump sum so that nobody can say with 100% certainty how much of the increase is available for any particular service. Nevertheless, you can see the gap in David Blunkett's claim.

Senior figures in the DFEE assured us that, although the Tories had habitually announced increases in the education SSA and then failed to provide the cash to back them, this government was different. The entire increase was fully funded, they claimed. However, research commissioned by Phil Willis from the House of Commons library shows that this claim is simply untrue. For the first year of Mr Blunkett's bonanza, 1999/2000, of the 150 local authorities in England, only four received an increase in TES cash which matched the increase in their notional SSA guideline for all services. The 146 others were all left with an increase which was part fact and part fiction. Twenty received so little extra cash that even if they ignored every other service and passed all of it to education, they would still not have enough new money to pay for the supposed increase in education alone. The government had announced an increase in SSA for all local services of £2.065 billion, but they actually provided only £1.5 billion. Contrary to their claims, they had funded only 73% of the total increase they were announcing.

For 1999/2000 Mr Blunkett claims, in the words of his original announcement, that 'government is providing' an increase of £1.1 billion for the LEAs. But if you look at the cash which the government is really providing in TES and, for the sake of clarity, assume that local authorities spread it equally across all their services, it turns out that the government is providing only £0.8 billion extra for education. Over the three years, the £3.6 billion guideline would turn out to be backed by only £2.6 billion of cash. The problem here is not simply that Mr Blunkett was misleading us when he claimed that the government was providing the extra money; worse, the evidence is that the local authorities will struggle to provide the missing cash themselves.

They can raise council tax, but the government has warned them that it will intervene if any of them raises local taxes too high. They can raid their reserves, as they did during the Tory years. Staffordshire, for example, spent £16.2 million of reserves on education; Leicestershire spent £13.7 million; Merton estimates it spent £30 million. But for several years now, increasing numbers of councils have been reporting that their reserves are running out. Or they can skim money off the top of their other budgets, particularly social services. This too was a common tactic in the Tory years, but this too is becoming increasingly difficult. In order to protect services for vulnerable children and old people, there is now real pressure at least to stop the skimming, and in some cases to reverse the flow and to start skimming the education budget to protect social services.

There is, nevertheless, on the face of it a cash increase of some £2.6 billion over three years in government funding for the LEAs. So the next question is how much of this money is new and not simply swallowed up by debt and rising costs?

Here, you need to understand that for years, Whitehall has been playing a game with the local authorities, holding down the SSA guidelines for education to a level so low that councillors were forced to spend more than the SSA in order to defend their schools – even if they were given no money to do so. This gap widened in the early 1990s to £2.9 billion a year – cash that the local education authorities were spending over and above the SSA guideline, even though the SSA guideline itself was not being fully funded by the Tories. But in the last six or seven years, more and more councils have been falling by the wayside, exhausted of extra cash, allowing their spending on education to slump back to the SSA level. This is the hidden story of Britain's education funding which is concealed by the talk of rising SSAs.

In 1992, according to figures supplied by the House of

Commons library, there were only two LEAs in England that were not spending above the SSA guidelines. By the time David Blunkett took office, there were thirty who had been forced below the SSA level. Behind the annual announcements of increases in SSA, the amount which the LEAs actually spent on education was falling steadily in real terms. In 1992/3, LEAs were spending £25.6 billion. Adjusted to 1992 prices, the figure fell sharply in the next year, to £21.8 billion. This was partly because further education was taken out of local authority control, but it was also part of a real funding fall which continued in every single subsequent year. In 1994/5, LEA spending dropped to £21.2 billion, then to £20.6 billion, then to £20.3 billion. And all this time, pupil numbers were rising. By the time Mr Blunkett announced his spending bonanza, his own department's figures showed that, in 1992 prices, the LEAs were spending only £19.9 billion; and, whereas they had once been spending £2.9 billion more than the SSA, they were now spending only £1.1 billion more than the Whitehall guideline. If Mr Blunkett wanted to avoid further cuts in LEA spending, he had to build any rise on top of the real level of spending, not on top of Whitehall's notional guideline. He chose not to. He ignored the entire shortfall of £1.1 billion in LEA funding.

On the face of it, he was steering the LEAs into disaster. If the extra cash he was giving them really amounted to only £0.8 for the first year, then all of this increase and more was going to be swallowed by this hungover annual debt. The reality is that LEAs have carried on clawing in extra money – but some of them have also carried on cutting. This year, the first of Mr Blunkett's bonanza, there are now fifty-three out of the 150 LEAs in England who are spending less than the SSA guideline on their schools. And all of the LEAs put together are now spending only £0.4 billion above the SSA guideline. There is no sign here of a reversal of fortune for the LEAs.

(In the summer of 1999 Mr Blunkett savaged LEAs for failing to 'passport' enough of their cash to schools, holding back too much for central administration. The LEAs said his figures were grossly misleading; Mr Blunkett continued to savage them. But that is a separate argument. The figures which have been falling are the total figure for LEA spending on education, whether it is passported to schools or spent on central services.)

It turns out that this lingering debt is only the first of a list of unacknowledged costs which will soak up Mr Blunkett's limited extra cash. This was spelled out to Mr Blunkett's department at the end of last year when local education authorities in England and Wales submitted a report – which the *Guardian* has seen – in which they explained in black and white that they did not have enough cash for the coming financial year, 2000/1. Mr Blunkett was suggesting (as part of his £3.6 billion increase in SSA over three years) that they spend an extra £1.211 billion for the year and that this would allow them to raise standards, but the LEAs complained that – even supposing they had enough cash to fund this increase in SSA – it would not allow them even to cover debts and unavoidable changes in their basic costs.

To close the remaining gap between SSA guidelines and real spending, the report said, they would need £388 million; plus £250 million for ordinary price inflation; £140 million for an increase in pupil numbers; £20 million for an increase in children with special needs; £125 million for an increase in employer contributions for teacher pensions; and £150 million for Mr Blunkett's new pay incentives for the best teachers. That long list left them with an increase of only £138 million for the year. And they had still allowed nothing for the annual teachers' pay rise (which has since been costed by Mr Blunkett at nearly £400 million); and, crucially, nothing at all to fund any improvement in standards. Mr Blunkett's officials disputed some of the numbers, but the embarrassing fact remained that right in the middle of Mr Blunkett's widely advertised three-year bonanza, the education authorities were heading for the red.

If you bear in mind that LEAs are not just partners but the sole source of mainstream budgets for schools, this was not only a financial problem for schools but a nasty political problem for Mr Blunkett. One official described the atmosphere in the department simply as 'panic'. The LEAs were particularly alarmed that they were being expected to take £150 million out of their inadequate budgets to pay for the new pay incentives for teachers, even though they had been promised that this scheme would be funded separately. And so it was that – without explaining any of this background – Mr Blunkett wrote to MPs on 26 November 1999 to announce an increase of £64 million in grant and a £90 million delay in school contributions to teacher pensions. This was a radical shift in plans – an emergency move. 'It was a complete surprise,' according to Neil Fletcher, head of education at the Local Government Association, 'although we were glad they admitted that their figures were wrong.'

There is no torrent of cash flooding through the mainstream of education; essentially, the same old drought continues. In Buckinghamshire, for example, in 1999, the local authority surveyed the state of local schools and found they would need a 13% real increase to meet their needs for teachers and other running costs, but Mr Blunkett's three-year increase gave them scarcely enough to allow school budgets to match rising costs. Looking at their buildings, they found they needed £6 million a year for repairs; they could afford only £2 million; and the backlog of building work had reached £21 million. Any plan to meet the needs of their schools, the council concluded, was 'unlikely to be achievable' within Mr Blunkett's spending limits. When the Association of Teachers and Lecturers surveyed a third of the schools in England and Wales last summer, they found that more than 2,000 teachers were about to lose their jobs for financial reasons, while others were holding on only because schools were spending reserves, cutting part-time hours and shedding support staff.

Some local authorities are claiming that, allowing for rising costs, there is simply no real new money for them at all. The system is constructed so as to make it impossible finally to prove or disprove the claim. The funding of local government is notoriously complex and produces irrational discrepancies between similar areas, and so it may be that some local education authorities will receive real, new cash from central government, but it is clear that the £3.6 billion boost which Mr Blunkett advertised is a political mirage.

There remains one final category – £3.3 billion of direct spending by the Department for Education. Here, at last, there is real additional money, unclouded by hyperbole or conjuring. Here, at last, there is some ground for Mr Blunkett to congratulate himself. And yet, even here, the story is not quite the one that he likes to tell.

Part of this direct spending does not go on education at all. It pays for Ofsted and for the central running costs of the DFEE. The department is the only area of British education which is exempt from the scrutiny and regulation which it has imposed on those below it, and local authorities have complained that while the department canes them for spending no more than 3% of their budget on central costs, the department spends nearly 7% of its own budget on its own administration, a trend it has seemed reluctant to admit. For example, when Phil Willis asked how much of the budget for Education Action Zones had been spent on administration, he was told the answer was £500,000. When he asked a few weeks later how much of the budget for EAZs had been spent on a specific list of administrative activities, he was told the answer was £1.14 million – nearly 10% of the entire EAZ budget. Willis went on to discover that the DFEE's spending on consultants has soared by more than £2 million during the current year, and that a single conference to discuss the New Deal for Schools in Birmingham had cost the DFEE more than a quarter of a million pounds.

The element of spending which does represent a real increase in spending is targeted grants – the Sure Start scheme for pre-schoolers, the programme to reduce class sizes, Education Action Zones and, most important, the Standards Fund (SF), a rapidly expanding collection of cash which is parcelled out by the department on some of Mr Blunkett's most high-profile projects including the literacy and numeracy schemes, the training of 'superheads', the programme to reduce truancy and exclusion, and the National Grid for Learning plan to provide computers for all schools. This year's Standards Fund is worth about £700 million, an increase of £300 million over last year. Next year it is due to rise by a further £400 million, with a comparable rise expected in the final year of the Parliament. During the three years of Mr Blunkett's bonanza, it will have risen by about £1 billion. This money is real, it is new, and, although it accounts for only about 5% of the cash received by schools, we found when we surveyed LEAs that it was cited repeatedly as a life-raft in the ocean of debt. However, there are two real problems with the way in which Mr Blunkett has administered the grants.

The first is that this system of grants not only bypasses the school budgets which are the core of education, but actually steals money away from them. This is because LEAs have to pay for most SF grants by providing up to 60% of their own matching funds: for almost every pound they accept from SF, they have to find up to 60 pence from somewhere else in their budget. This year, they are expected to pay out £400 million in matching funds. Next year, as the SF rises, they face a bill of £600 million. Almost all of the LEAs who replied to our survey reported that they were struggling as a result. Brent has decided to turn down grants in order to protect the budgets of its schools; Islington says it has accepted the grants but may have to start top-slicing its school budgets to find the matching funds; Cheshire has already cut its school budgets by 5% to pay for SF grants; Derbyshire has had to divert £1.8 million from its school budgets; Stockport has had to cut its central services by £360,000. The director of education in Worcestershire, Julian Kramer, told us that as a result of pressure from the Standards Fund 'we can point to significant evidence of schools who are cash-strapped for almost everything except training'.

The second problem is that this money is failing to reach the most needy schools. The department has consistently claimed that it wants to provide, in the words of Schools Minister Estelle Morris, 'targeted support for the areas of poverty'. There are one or two programmes, like Excellence in Cities, which are specifically focused on deprived areas. However, most SF grants are distributed on a simple formula which takes no account of deprivation and the rest, as well as grants for some repairs, are distributed on a bidding system. When the former Lib Dem education spokesman, Don Foster, extracted figures from the department, he found that there was no correlation at all between successful bids and areas of poverty. Indeed, the richer authorities tended to do better, apparently because they had more staff and resources to prepare their bids.

Don Foster found that schools with the most affluent pupils (less than 10% eligible for free meals) were receiving grants worth between £326 and £1,264 per pupil, while schools with the most deprived pupils (more than 40% eligible for free meals) were receiving no more than £791 per pupil. Local authorities in affluent areas, like Rutland and the Isles of Scilly (both with only 6.4% eligible for free meals), had reaped more than £1,000 per pupil, while areas like Sunderland or Sefton, with four times the rate of eligibility for free meals, had been given only £298 and £317 respectively. There was no match between the funding and the need for it. As a DFEE official explained at a Treasury workshop last year: 'The simple truth is that those who start with an advantage are usually better placed to exploit any new system.'

Foster's research also revealed that overstretched schools and local authorities were wasting considerable time and money in unsuccessful bids. During Mr Blunkett's first two years there were 25,353 bids, but only 8,972 were successful. Oxfordshire made 1,015 bids and saw 1,002 of them fail. Blackpool put in 212 bids and succeeded with only 10. These figures were shocking partly because of the unfulfilled need which they indicated, but also because of the scarce resources which were being lost in the bid process. In many cases, Foster found, local authorities had hired consultants who would skim 10% off the top of any grant they succeeded in landing.

The torrent of new money turns out to be little more than a trickle, with new cash being soaked up so fast that it scarcely leaves its mark. You can see this in the experience of St Giles' primary school in Coventry, where they won a grant from the Standards Fund to buy fifteen new computers – and then had no money to make the IT room secure or even to pay for the sockets to plug them in. Eventually they raised extra funds with bingo and a Christmas Fayre. You can see it on a larger scale in one of Mr Blunkett's proudest achievements, the

100

highly successful scheme to cut the size of classes for infants aged five to seven. By 1999 the Prime Minister was pointing to impressive results, with 100,000 more infants in classes of under thirty. What the Prime Minister did not say was that children in every other age bracket – nursery, junior and secondary – were all being taught in classes that were even more overcrowded than when New Labour came to power. Last year's figures showed the number of children in classes of more than forty had doubled since David Blunkett took over; the number in secondary classes of more than thirty was the worst for fourteen years; secondary classes generally were more overcrowded than they had been for twenty years.

And this trickle of new money over the last three years of the Parliament is flowing into a system which was made marginally worse during Mr Blunkett's first two years. Despite Labour's election promise to make education their first priority, the department's share of government spending actually fell during these two years, from 11.8 to 11.7%. Ten years earlier, when Kenneth Baker was running the department, he had put 12.3% of government spending into education. By the end of Mr Blunkett's first year, spending per secondary pupil, in real terms, had fallen from £2,550 in 1992 to only £2,380. During his second year, spending in real terms was frozen while pupil numbers rose, with the result that spending per secondary pupil fell to its lowest since 1989. Looking back at Blunkett's first two years, the Educational Publishers Council reported in 1999 that Britain was providing its pupils with only £18 worth of books each year, less than any other country in Western Europe.

The reality is that while Mr Blunkett is entitled to point to his increase in Standards Fund and other central grants as a real bounty for British education, almost all of the rest of his £19 billion is an illusion, and the grants alone have not begun to reverse the historic underfunding of Britain's schools and its aggravation during his first two years. The idea that his original announcement of the bonanza was an historic day which would 'give everyone in our society the opportunity to realise their full potential' was just another flourish from the man with the magic wand.

WHAT'S WRONG WITH PRIVATE SCHOOLS?

8 MARCH 2000

LET US BEGIN with the story of what the historian Professor Brian Simon once described as 'probably the biggest hijack of public resources in history'. This was plotted more than 100 years ago, in 1869, when the government's Schools Inquiry Commission declared that there was no reason to encourage 'indiscriminate gratuitous instruction', an idea they compared in its mischief to the indiscriminate donation of alms to beggars. They proposed an ingenious reform, which was rapidly adopted by Parliament. First they would seize the schools which then provided a free education for the poor in many towns; then (ignoring the statutes which had established them) they would abolish them; and then (defying the lawful wishes of their benefactors) they would take over the endowments which had been left over the years to fund them and use the money to set up schools not for the poor but 'for the extension of middle class education'.

This was a bold idea, for which the commissioners received much credit, but in truth it was not an original one. For centuries the masters of the great public schools had been enriching their institutions by the same device. All of these schools were founded for the free education of the poor – that is why they were originally called 'public' schools. When Henry VI founded Eton in 1442, for example, he instructed that 'No one having a yearly income of more than five marks shall be eligible.' In 1382, the founder of Winchester, William of Wykeham, declared that the school was to be made up of seventy 'poor and needy' pupils, although as a concession to

102

those whose patronage he sought he agreed also to take ten 'sons of noble and influential persons'. Rugby, Harrow, Westminster – they were all founded as free schools for the poor. Yet all of them eventually were hijacked by the wealthy, who paid fees to attend. The headmasters were happy to take their money, and were inventive in helping the hijack.

Thomas Arnold preserved Rugby for the rich by closing its free lower school, so that, unless the children of the poor could afford to pay someone else to teach them, they could not learn enough to get into the main school. The schools insisted that new pupils should be able to speak Latin, with the same result. At Harrow the head man took the register at noon, when the poorer pupils, who were day boys, were all at home for lunch; just to make sure of their absence, he forbade them from riding horses to speed up their journey home. Westminster wriggled out of its legal obligation to the poor by arguing that Queen Elizabeth I had never confirmed its statutes. Winchester justified its behaviour to the 1818 Brougham Commission by explaining that, in truth, its current pupils really were poor – it was only their parents who were rich.

With the Public Schools Act of 1868, these ancient schools completed the theft by capturing any remaining endowments which were still dedicated to poor pupils. A year later, following the lead of the Schools Inquiry Commission, the Endowed Schools Act organised a far grander larceny, seizing from towns all over the country a fortune in endowments which had been left for the benefit of the local poor but which were now used to pay for a network of new fee-paying private schools for the middle class. As a single example, Sutton Coldfield, whose poor had been educated for free by virtue of endowment, saw £15,000 taken from them to provide 'a high school for well to do children' – and a further £17,000 for a high school for girls. There were petitions and protests, but the affluent had their way. The poor were left only with the bare bones of an 'elementary education' granted them by the 1870 Education Act. They never saw their money again.

Now we come forward a century and look at the state of Britain's schools during the last twenty years. From twisted roots, a mighty structure has grown – 2,300 private schools with an annual income from fees of some £3.2 billion, educating nearly 600,000 pupils, a magnificent 7% of the nation's children. This remains the most unusual feature of the educational landscape of Britain. There are other countries that allow private schools to operate alongside their state system – almost every developed democracy does. There are some that educate far more of their children in private schools (17% in France, 13% in Denmark). However, apart from small pockets of privilege, invariably these are religious schools, like those in France or Italy, or 'free' schools like those in Denmark, often underfunded and relying on state subsidy to survive. There is no other country in Europe where private schools present a fully-fledged alternative to the state system, open essentially only to the affluent.

Does that matter? In the first instance, it is a question of power. Stephen Pollard and Andrew Adonis, now a Downing Street adviser, recorded in their book, *A Class Act*, that on the latest available figures the magnificent 7% accounted for: seven out of nine senior generals; thirty-three out of thirty-nine of the most senior judges; more than 120 of the 180 officers graduating from Sandhurst; half of the eighteen permanent secretaries running Whitehall; and just under half of the ninety-four Grade Three civil servants then aged under fifty (most of the rest went to grammar schools, some of which have since been privatised). Research for the Economic and Social Research Council found that 75% of private school pupils went on to take professional or managerial jobs. From the state schools, 40% reached that level.

This question of power, and of social justice, has ceased to be fashionable, largely because the politics which kept the question alive have been marginalised. However, in a pragmatic age an equally pressing version of the question remains – a purely educational one. The debate about the desirability of our private schools has hardly ever been framed in this way. The question is: does the existence of private schools have any impact on the educational performance of the mainstream state system? Can we relax and allow the two systems to enjoy a peaceful coexistence or is there some kind of destructive friction between the two? The answer is not quite what you might expect.

Consider, for example, the hiring and firing of teachers in the state and private system, a subject which has tended to remain encased in privacy but which has been unlocked by the research of Simon Szreter, an economic historian at St John's College, Cambridge. Szreter analysed World Development Reports and found that in the last twenty years, Britain had fallen behind just about every other developed country in its investment in teachers for the state sector. Meanwhile, the private schools had forged ahead.

All through the 1970s, Szreter found, both state schools and private schools in the UK had followed the behaviour of all developed countries in hiring extra teachers, and by the end of the decade the combined efforts of the Heath, Wilson and Callaghan governments had put an extra 100,000 teachers on the payroll. State schools were closing the gap on private schools: whereas at the beginning of the decade the average state class contained twenty-six children, by 1979 it contained only nineteen. The private schools were still placed better – their pupil:teacher ration was about 50% lower – and the average of nineteen disguised a mass of state classes of more than thirty, sometimes more than forty, but the state sector was clearly catching up. Then Mrs Thatcher took over.

By demographic chance, in the 1980s pupil numbers started to fall, in both private and state schools, but while the private sector continued to invest in more teachers, the new Conservative administration took advantage of the falling pupil numbers to get rid of them. During the 1980s, half of the extra teachers who had been hired in the 1970s – 50,000 of them – were removed from the payroll. The fall in pupils meant that the pupil:teacher ratio dropped for a while and then, as pupil numbers rose again, it climbed back. Szreter found that all of Britain's main economic competitors had continued to invest heavily in teachers: 'By 1991, the best of continental countries were running a ratio of between ten and twelve pupils per teacher.' But Britain's state schools were still stuck with an average of nineteen students in every classroom. In the early 1990s, only four of the twenty-five most developed societies had larger classes than Britain – Ireland, Hong Kong, Singapore and South Korea – and Szreter suspects that when the figures are finally brought up to date, they may well all have left Britain behind: 'No other democratically elected government in the modern world has dreamed up this masterstroke of actually disinvesting in the educational resources of the nation.'

In the meantime, the private schools had continued hiring and re-established their superiority, with average classes containing only ten pupils, nearly 100% lower than the state. Szreter estimates that to regain a position where the state school classes are only 50% larger than private ones, the government would need to hire 100,000 new teachers.

Clearly, there is real unfairness in this. Yet that does not, on the face of it, entitle us to blame the private schools. Where is the evidence that this mass shedding of teachers happened because there was a system of private schools over the fence and not simply because a Conservative government was intent on cutting public spending in order to fund tax cuts? There are more clues deeper in the background. The reversal in the staffing of state schools was part of a wider picture of encroaching financial hardship. Although the Conservatives often increased the notional annual SSA guideline for spending on education, they invariably failed to provide enough cash to keep pace with inflation and pupil numbers and, in spite of waves of protest from parents and teachers, they allowed the real-terms funding of state schools to shrink.

In the London borough of Ealing, for example, the local education authority dug into its reserves, switched money from other budgets, but nevertheless was compelled to cut. Ealing's director of education, Alan Parker, reconstructed what happened. To begin with, he says, the borough protected its schools and cut the support services: eight education welfare officers were lost, just as the demand for their work on truancy and exclusion was rising; the Education Psychology Service was cut to the point where, instead of offering help to schools, it could do little more than prepare statements to get funding for children with special needs; the number of staff who could teach English as a foreign language was halved. The pressure persisted and the borough was forced to cut its adult education. Now there were grants for higher education and Further Education only for those on income support who chose to pursue one of a narrow range of vocational courses; the rest would have to fund themselves or forget it. The youth service was cut by 50%. Arts, libraries and museums, too. Routine maintenance of buildings fell to zero – 'one of the main scandals of the period' according to Parker. Then the cuts reached inside the schools – no more tuition in music, larger classes, less administrative support, less for books, less for classroom equipment, less for materials. 'It is self-evidently the case,' Alan Parker concludes, 'that the overall experience of education has been impoverished as a result.'

Our survey of LEAs produced similar accounts from all over the country. State schools found themselves caught in a pincer, compelled by law to teach the national curriculum, but compelled by cuts to reduce their service. The result, as our survey showed, was that LEAs and schools cut back on music, sports, French in primary schools, libraries, special schools, outdoor centres – anything that was not protected by law was liable to be cut. This was not a case of losing unwanted fat.

In one year of John Major's spending limits, Merton, who have drawn some £30 million out of reserves, nevertheless had to cut their education budget by £4.7 million, most of which came directly from the budgets of schools, who responded by cutting staff and reducing maintenance on their buildings. The London borough of Hammersmith has had to cut its budget for schools every year for the last six years, taking a total of £2.5 million from them. Derbyshire has lost teachers in each of the last eight years, a total of 1,361. When Ofsted inspected Northumberland's LEA recently, they found that the council's income had fallen in real terms every year from 1992 to 1998, with the result that, despite the council's efforts to protect them, their schools had suffered an 11% cut in budgets while central spending on education had been cut by 36%. Since the late 1980s, budgets for secondary schools in Cheshire have fallen in real terms by 6%; student awards were cut from £9 million to only £0.5 million; adult education was cut by 30%. Staffordshire education had to cut £9 million out of its education spending. And on and on.

It was in the course of this long period of attrition that Mrs Thatcher proclaimed: 'I do not care what people's background is, where they come from. I want them to have the same opportunities, I want to get totally rid of class distinction.' By 1991, two thousand state schools were contacting the BBC's Children in Need project in search of money to repair buildings and hire more teachers.

The private schools, however, were doing well, and part of the reason for this was that, with almost nineteenth-century logic, they were receiving a very healthy subsidy from the state. Despite protests from the Labour Party, the Conservative government continued to allow many private schools to enjoy the status of charity. This meant that they escaped all tax on income from stocks, shares, trusts and property, as well as escaping all VAT, corporation tax on their profit, capital gains tax and stamp duty on their property transactions, inheritance tax on their new endowments and up to 100% of their business rates.

In 1996, the Independent Schools Council (ISC) surveyed 838 of its members and concluded that they were saving £62.6 million a year. In 1992, however, the Master of Haileybury, David Jewell, suggested that if private schools lost their charitable status, fees would have to rise by up to 30%. This suggested that their tax break was a great deal more valuable: those at the top end of Mr Jewell's estimate would be receiving more financial support from the state than the state schools themselves. For the average ISC school, a tax break of 30% of their fees would mean they were receiving a state subsidy of some £1,945 per pupil – some £200 a year more than the state now invests in the education of a child at primary school. The average boarding school pupil would be enjoying an annual subsidy from the taxpayer of £3,760 – 60% more than the state pays for its own secondary pupils. In the top boarding schools, a tax break of that scale would grant the richest students twice the support from public funds which is currently provided for state secondary students. No one knows how accurate this picture may be. Neither the government, the schools nor the charities commission has ever produced the figures.

The private schools also continued to benefit from state money through the Ministry of Defence, which pays fees for the children of some personnel (currently running at £72 million a year), and also through the Foreign Office, which similarly pays fees for the children of some staff (currently £12.5 million a year). Arguably, they also enjoy an unrecognised subsidy in the universities, which are used disproportionately by children from private schools. Almost 90% of private pupils go on to higher education – more than 20% of all university entrants.

All this subsidy was already in place when Mrs Thatcher became Prime Minister. However, in 1981 she introduced a new and even more lucrative form of support, the Assisted Places Scheme, which paid the fees of up to 36,000 pupils a year – some boarders and some day – thus providing the private schools with a guaranteed income from the state of nearly £900 million during the Conservative years. In this way, new money flowed through the same old channels that had been dug more than a hundred years before, from the education of the poor towards the well-to-do, and in increasingly large amounts.

This financial aid was only one part of the bounty which the state now bestowed on the private-sector schools. There was a time when these two systems were effectively sealed off from each other as each generation of children divided to follow the footsteps of its parents, but this era saw the growth in schools of the One Big Market. Because the spending cuts were hurting the performance and reputation of state schools; because the income from fees and state subsidy was pushing the private schools still further ahead; because the Conservatives were cutting tax and putting more money into middle-class pockets, enabling them to buy their way into private schools; because private schools saw it was financially and politically wise to invest in a wider range of pupils; because Kenneth Baker gave parents the right to choose state schools for their children; and because he then ordered that the funding should follow the children into the most popular schools, thus further damaging the reputation and performance of 'failing' schools – for all these reasons the number of children in private schools began to rise.

When Mrs Thatcher came to power, only 5.8% of the nation's children were in the private sector; by the time she left, the number had risen to 7%. In Greater London, 12% of the children were in private schools. There was no doubt about where these children were coming from: according to the ISC, most parents who now send their children to private schools were themselves educated in the state sector. In many other ways, the two sectors of schooling remained separate; there were still many pupils who were born into one sector and could not conceive of entering the other; but in the centre, in this commercial sense, the private schools and the state schools had been pulled together, in competition with each other in the market for pupils. To reinforce the trend, the Conservatives encouraged state schools to opt out of LEA control, taking extra funds to become grant-maintained schools with the power to select their intake.

As all this evidence unfolds, a clearer answer begins to emerge to the question of coexistence. No other country in Europe has a full-fledged alternative to its state schools. No other country in Europe 'disinvested' in its state schools. And what about the people who were responsible for this disinvestment? Almost without exception, the ministers who increased the size of state classes, and who assured everyone that it made no difference to the quality of education, then chose to send their own children to be educated in private schools which had spent a small fortune cutting the size of their classes. This is not simply a point about jealousy, that it was not fair. It has broad implications about politics.

In his book, *We Should Know Better*, the former Tory education minister, George Walden, argues with considerable authority that Britain's state schools have suffered persistent negligence because the power elite has had no interest in protecting them. He writes: 'The screening out of the sons and daughters of the affluent and influential from the rest of society . . . and the consequent indifference of their parents to

110

what goes on in state schools is more than a traditional quirk in the English system. It severs our educational culture at the neck . . . No country has evolved a high standard of public education while the top seven per cent of its citizens have nothing to do with it.'

In this crucial sense, the history of Britain's education, from the birth of the old public schools through the hijacking of the free schools for the poor and the more recent diversion of favour from state to private during the Conservative era, is precisely a story about the private sector actively damaging the state sector, by providing for the children of the rich and powerful a safe haven which leaves the state schools with only the most meagre political protection. In this sense, the coexistence never has been peaceful. Beyond this, the creation of the One Big Market has now introduced a second and equally important kind of damage: on a scale they have never achieved before, the private schools are skimming bright children off the top of the state system.

In 1993, the National Commission for Education spotted the underlying trend in Britain's schools. Contrary to popular legend, this was not that Britain's system was in a state of collapse, or that standards were so much lower than the rest of the world. The trend was in the gaps between the best and the worst: 'The gulf in outcomes between our best schools and our worst is big, much bigger than in most countries. The OECD . . . found that differences between English schools in levels of mathematical achievement were far larger than in any of the ten other countries studied, including Scotland, with the single exception of Switzerland.'

This is all about polarisation. That commission specifically warned about the potential damage caused by Kenneth Baker's introduction, five years earlier, of an effective market in school places. We described in the first part of this series how those reforms had created a two-tier system of state schools: the successful school in the affluent suburb attracting more and more motivated, middle-class pupils and more and more funds; while the failing school down the road became a ghetto, starved of motivated children, penalised by the loss of funds. Every time a government boosts the private schools, it

111

reinforces that process of polarisation. The fact that the private schools run explicitly on a system of academic selection means that there is no ambiguity at all about what is happening (in the way that there may be some marginal ambiguity with the middle-class state school): they are taking the brightest children. Which, in itself, adds another twist to the polarisation, by advancing their own academic results and depressing those of the state.

As a single example, take Bedfordshire, where according to County Councillor Tony Mitchell, 12% of the county's brightest children are skimmed off by four private schools in the Harpur Trust. Councillor Mitchell, a former teacher and now a school governor, said: 'In the heyday of the grammar school, a county like Essex selected only six per cent of the ability range.' In addition, the Conservatives' grant-maintained schools, with extra funding from LEAs, select pupils and skim a further 27% of Bedfordshire children. 'Some schools, all in areas of disadvantage, are threatened with closure while one GM school has 54% of its pupils from outside its catchment area.'

Yet this does not quite conclude the argument. Events have moved on. The year after George Walden wrote his book, New Labour came to power. In its strange insecurity towards conservative Britain, it has drawn little attention to the fact that in among its rhetoric of partnership with the private schools, it has dealt them two rather painful body blows. This was the result apparently of a compromise with the party's former radical position. David Blunkett in particular had argued with some passion, when Labour were in opposition, that the private schools must be stripped of their charitable status. In 1994, for example, he complained publicly that 'all of us are paying for someone else to get a privileged education'. He lost the policy battle but he persisted in his efforts to impose VAT on private school fees. He lost that battle, too, and yet he did not lose the whole war.

One of Mr Blunkett's first steps as education secretary was to kill off the Assisted Places Scheme. By the time he entered his first full year of power, 1997/98, the scheme had become a fat cash cow, delivering an annual £134.4 million pounds to

112

the private schools. Mr Blunkett killed it, was sued in the High Court, was heavily criticised but stuck to the policy. Then he introduced tuition fees in universities. It was a move that hurt almost all potential students. It also hurt the private schools by diverting some of the parental cash which might otherwise have gone into private sixth forms. In the background, the collapse of economies in East Asia, whose affluent elite had become a source of succour for the private schools, delivered a third blow.

There are now signs of struggle in the private sector. The Independent Schools Council reported in 1999 that the number of children at its schools had increased by 0.71%, but that disguised the real trend. The increase consists entirely of a surge in children going to private nurseries, while the numbers taking both GCSEs and A levels has started to fall. More than that, there has been a steady and ultimately drastic fall in the flow of the most lucrative pupils, the boarders: in 1983, 27.7% of ISC pupils were boarders; last year it was only 14.9%. Last year alone, the number of boarders fell by 4.3%. In the 1980s, the schools found new boarders by opening their doors to girls, a novelty they cannot now repeat; and by pulling in far more students from abroad. But last year, the foreigners, too, began to turn their backs, their numbers falling by 1.4%.

In summer 1999, City accountants Pricewaterhouse Coopers reported that scores of private schools were likely to close in the next decade. Thirteen per cent of schools in their survey were running a deficit, many had been hurt by the removal of Assisted Places, they reported, and small schools for girls were particularly vulnerable. Richard Davison of the ISC said: 'It is a free market and the weaker schools are going. It's the ones who are very small, or who rely too much on boarders, or who have rural locations. They are vulnerable. Once you move away from the top schools, it is brutal.'

While Winchester and Westminster may soak up the applause at centre stage, off in the wings there are some deeply troubled private schools, suffering with an intake of poorly motivated children and very low fees. Ofsted's annual report in 1997/8 pointed out that while 10% of private schools see every single pupil scoring at least five A to C grades at GCSE, there are 5% of private schools who cannot score a single A to C grade for any of their pupils. That year, they inspected only 411 private schools, but 60 'caused considerable concern'. School inspectors reported:

Only one teacher has qualified teacher status . . . classrooms are unsafe and unhealthy and so unfit for the education of children . . . excessive shouting at children, and signs of distress shown by several children as a result . . . failure to carry out the required checks on newly appointed staff . . . failure to keep records of instances of corporal punishment . . . overall the quality of education is poor . . . the school is failing to provide a properly broad and balanced education for its pupils at any stage . . . a school in decline, which is poorly managed on severely limited resources . . . the air of decay . . . the lack of resources . . . low paid teachers and a high turnover in particular subjects . . .

The private schools can see the threat and they are all suddenly buzzing like flies around old meat, desperately looking for some new device to secure their position. Some have been forced into a dangerous hike in their fees. A survey by Mintel, the market research groups, last year found that in the previous year, fees had risen by 5.2% while inflation was only 3.3%. Others have launched financial appeals, the weak looking for survival and the strong looking for even more strength. Stowe School in Buckingham, for example, is trying to win an edge over Uppingham by raising £6 million for a new Academic Resource Centre, a computerised library and audio-visual centre, electronically linked to classrooms. But Uppingham has already laid fifty miles of cabling through its sixteenth-century buildings and is claiming to have one of the most sophisticated ICT systems in the country, with 1,500 terminals for its 650 pupils. Others are investing in sport – golf courses are big, for example – and Eton is raising more than £3 million (much of it through the Lottery) to pay for a new music centre, arts complex and boating lake.

Where once private schools marketed themselves by

sending the head teacher to preach in an outside church, the big private players are now playing the market game professionally. Two hundred and eighty private schools have formed the Association of Development Directors in Independent Schools (ADDIS). Their chair, Felicity Rutland, told us: 'Marketing professionals are no longer a luxury, they are key members of the school's management team.' Many of them have already adapted to fit their markets. When the number of boarders fell, they abandoned tradition and let in girls; when middle-class parents objected to the cane, almost all of them banned it before Parliament forced them to. There are now real niche markets – and friction between them. An overtly liberal head warned us that 'the hothouse atmosphere' in some of the most famous schools was damaging some children by marking them as failures, and that 'There is a vast rank of top and middling schools which are still in the nineteenth century, modelled on the army, named after generals, strong on uniform – and on children being uniform. Parents send their children there so the child won't have to sit next to a dustman's child, and they celebrate all the great moral certainties of Victorian Britain – the Anglican Church, Kipling, not speaking out.' Conservative head teachers are equally disparaging of some of their competition.

As demand for their places has fallen, smaller schools have started to lower their entrance hurdles. It is an irony that the education pundits who criticise the very idea of comprehensive schooling and look with admiration on private schools fail to see that the biggest comprehensives in the country are in the private sector – and they are also the most successful because they are properly funded: Rugby, for example, is regarded by many private head teachers as a model comprehensive with a very wide range of academic ability, a living example of what can happen when a comprehensive is given enough money to do its job.

In theory, the government that was willing to kill off the Assisted Places Scheme might have continued to defend the state schools in the One Big Market, allowing them to punch their weight in the marketplace. Indeed, in theory, that is what government policy is supposed to be. As the Prime

Minister put it in his *Channel 4 News* interview last autumn: 'The best answer to the public schools is to develop state education of really high quality, and changes in fact are of course happening now.'

In terms of their funding, however, the disparity between private and state remains breath taking. Last year, ISC found that their schools were charging on average £5,460 for a year, while state schools were receiving from all sources an average total of only £2,732 per pupil. To put it another way – setting aside tax breaks and other subsidies – pupils in state schools are receiving only 43% of the funding which is enjoyed by private school pupils. Bear in mind also that some of the most successful private schools receive a considerable income from investments and property which they can add to their income from fees, so that a school like Eton can spend some £20,000 a year on each of its pupils.

In contrast to the scything cuts in music, French and sport in the state primary schools, a survey in 1999 by the Incorporated Association of Preparatory Schools found that 93% of private prep schools teach music, most of them with specialist teachers in specialist rooms; almost all of them teach French; two-thirds teach Latin; a quarter teach German; one in seven teaches Spanish; and they enjoy an average of 18.3 acres of land, the equivalent of nine full-sized football pitches each. Since 1981, state schools have been forced to sell more than 5,000 playing fields. Although Labour promised to end the sale, they are still being sold off at a rate of about twenty a year.

While private schools had been installing computers and linking them to the Internet and their own internal Intranets, the state primary schools in 1998 were providing only one computer for every eighteen pupils; only 17% of them were linked to the Internet. In secondary schools there was one computer between nine pupils. By that time private schools, like Bedales in Hampshire, for example, were leasing laptops to their students and aiming to provide one computer for each pupil. In an attempt to catch up, David Blunkett invested £310 million in the National Grid for Learning and saw the figures start to climb in 1999.

The end result of all this is a system on the edge of despair. Craven Park Primary School in north London is so short of money that when the filter on its swimming pool breaks down it is forced to close the whole pool permanently. A successful comprehensive – one of the government's favoured Beacon Schools – holds a sponsored spelling contest to raise money for GCSE textbooks. While David Blunkett tries to cut classes for infants down to thirty, the Dutch have pledged to cut classes for all children – to twenty. Since Mr Blunkett's claim to be spending an extra £19 billion has collapsed in empty rhetoric, state schools literally cannot compete. They cannot raise or lower their fees, and their capacity to raise funds is much inferior. Their efforts so far speak more of their current desperation than their prospective wealth.

Many have turned to their parents. The National Council of PTAs has said its members are raising an average of £3,000 for their schools and that most of it is being spent not on new attractions but on essentials – the repair of buildings and the supply of classroom equipment. Mayfield Primary School in Cambridgeshire has been asking parents for £10 a month in an attempt to keep classes below thirty. Parents there have also been decorating classrooms and building a playground. The head teacher, Jaspaul Hill, said: 'I do not feel right to be asking for donations. Our governing body does not feel it is right. It does not rest easily at all.'

Teachers too have become funders. When the Association of Teachers and Lecturers surveyed its members two years ago, it found that half of them had dug into their own pockets to buy resources for the literacy hour which was supposed to have been fully funded by the Department for Education. The association reckoned that a fifth of their members had paid out more than £50 and that in total, across the country, primary school teachers had probably put as much as £5 million of their own cash into filling the gaps in funding in the campaign.

Corporations, sensing an opportunity, have moved to fill the gap. The National Consumer Council reported three years ago that industry was spending £300 million a year on sponsorship aimed at schools, but they found many sponsors had been quite unable to resist the temptation to promote their own products. Cadbury's, for example, produced free sheets in which they mentioned themselves fifty-five times and told pupils as a 'chocolate fact' that 'chocolate is a wholesome food . . . [and] gives you energy and important nutrients that your body needs to work properly.' Whiskas produced a booklet called *Know Your Cat* and advised children that 'a steady diet of Whiskas kitten food provides a properly balanced source of nutrition for your kitten'. McDonald's produced teaching packs for English, maths and geography for infants in which they used McDonald's fries and milk-shakes as images for matching, and planted their own name in a word puzzle. British Nuclear Fuel produced a leaflet on *Energy and the Environment* in which they made no mention of nuclear waste remaining dangerous for many thousands of years and, after referring to the devastating accident at Chernobyl, continued: 'Accidents happen all the time. Can you think of some accidents that have happened in school, at home, or locally?'

Beyond this weakness of resources, the failure of the state schools' marketing and management is even more pronounced. While parts of the private sector are graduating into the slick world of educational one-upmanship, the DFEE is still in kindergarten, making little palm prints in bright red paint. It is one of the central paradoxes of New Labour's approach to education that they have preserved the market in schools which was created by Kenneth Baker, they have embraced the culture of private enterprise, and yet they have imposed a rigid old-fashioned regime of centrist diktat which means that schools and LEAs are quite unable to respond to the market in any creative way. While most private schools are free of Ofsted inspections, compulsory SATs tests and the national curriculum, state schools are free to adapt neither to the children in their classrooms nor to the market beyond. The old maxim that Britain's state schools are centrally funded but locally delivered is collapsing: first, under the weight of the Standards Fund, which means that almost all spare cash is being directed from the centre; and second, under a torrent of central instruction. (In his first two years,

Mr Blunkett issued 322 directives to schools and LEAs and launched fifty-two centrally-managed initiatives.)

Even the department's most benevolent schemes suffer from central direction. In Ealing, for example, the drive to cut the size of infant classes to thirty backfired in a school which previously housed thirty-two infants in one class with a teacher and a classroom assistant. Forced to cut the number to thirty, the school found it could no longer afford the assistant and so ended up with more pupils per member of staff than when it started.

Few other businesses are guided by advisers who insist that investment is an optional extra. Giving evidence to the select committee on education, Chris Woodhead dismissed with contempt the idea that state teachers were suffering from a lack of resources: 'They blame the government for a lack of resources, they blame parents for not producing intelligent enough pupils, and they blame the collapse of Western civilisation as we know it.' This was on 3 November 1999. Six months earlier, the headmaster of Winchester, James Sabben-Clare, had told the *Daily Telegraph* that if independent schools were restricted to spending an average of £2,300 a year per pupil, as state schools are, the quality of education they could offer would be greatly diminished. Fees at Winchester run at £15,000 a year.

Few other businesses are marketed by managers who publicly denounce their product, attack their staff, savage their local managers, and sing the praises of the competition. No other organisation in the country is managed with the kind of organised public exposure which is experienced by schools and local education authorities. It is doubtful whether any other organisation – corporate boardroom, factory floor, legal chambers, newsroom – could survive that kind of scrutiny and denunciation. There are drunkards in alleys with a better strategy for self-advertisement.

All this means that the state schools remain highly vulnerable to the schools they are now encouraged to see as partners. The answer to the question of coexistence is that purely in educational terms, the private schools continue to inflict damage on the state sector, draining away political interest and bright pupils. Why does the DFEE not do more to protect them?

The former Tory education minister, George Walden, blamed some of the department's problems on low-calibre civil servants. He argued that top-flight officials went off to the high-prestige departments like the Foreign Office, leaving education in the hands of the also-rans: 'Able people have worked there, but on average the quality has not been commensurate with the importance of the work.' The problem, however, surely goes deeper than a mere shortage of managerial flair.

One of the battering rams used by critics to attack state schooling in the last twenty years has been a contempt for those who, in the words of Kenneth Baker, 'seek to use education for social engineering'. It is this which is held to have poisoned the well of state schooling by producing the comprehensive system. It is this perversion which is blamed for a 'levelling down' in the classroom.

Now go back, for a moment, to the Schools Inquiry Commission and look at its confident assertion that there was no justification for 'indiscriminate gratuitous instruction'. Well? Is there? The unemployed require no qualifications. Even skilled workers do not need A levels, let alone university degrees. The Conservative and National governments of the 1920s and 1930s understood this and resisted all efforts by the Labour Party to introduce universal secondary education and to raise the school leaving age. On the eve of the Second World War, working-class children in this country were still entitled only to 'elementary education' to the age of fourteen; 10% of them managed to graduate into county grammar schools or direct grant schools, often paying fees. And that was it.

The impetus to allow the working class into the higher reaches of education was and remains political and moral – it enables the workers not merely to work but to aspire to break out of their class and move upwards. In that sense, any move towards educating the working class is guilty of precisely the crime of which it is so frequently still accused by its conservative detractors – social engineering. If you deny the role

120

of social justice in education, you remove any logical justification for universal schooling. For all its humanity and social justice, it makes no economic sense at all. Any sane Treasury official, therefore, will resist it. Which is what they have done, very successfully.

The ideology of partnership has silenced talk of social justice in New Labour's education policy and so, in one simple sweep of rhetoric, more than a hundred years of development is left hanging. The point is not that the DFEE or its ministers are part of some conspiracy to undermine the state schools. The truth rather is that, in an age of pragmatism, they have lost their political philosophy and so they have no basis on which to fight a battle for public opinion to explain that they cannot fund a revival in state schools without raising taxes. They prefer to pretend that they have found the money, regardless of reality. In the same way, they will not challenge the received wisdom of the Conservative years but prefer to recycle the muddled half-truths of parental choice and funding formulae and Ofsted and league tables, offering no kind of leadership, no kind of insight, no kind of hope. And, in the meantime, the market continues to favour the strong.

R.H. Tawney, Labour Party thinker, said in *Equality*, in 1931: 'The hereditary curse upon English education is its organisation upon lines of social class.' Martin Stephens, High Master of Manchester Grammar School, one of the private schools which commands most admiration from the government, told us: 'We have created a system of almost total confusion . . . I would now find it easier to explain the rules of cricket to a European than I would the English educational system. It is basically a vision of chaos.'

THE DEBATE
David Blunkett replies

It takes a special kind of magic to obscure the best education settlement in decades in the manner of Nick Davies.

Let's start with an independent fact. The Institute of Fiscal Studies confirmed in its Green Budget that 'by 2002, Labour will have achieved an annualised real increase in education spending of 3.2%, double that of the last administration and more than twice that of the Conservatives over their entire term of office from 1979 to 1997'.

Sustained increases are going into schools in a way which never happened before. The Conservatives had a one-off increase in 1992 and cut spending afterwards. Real spending per pupil fell by £50 in the last three Conservative budgets. In contrast, there will be a real-terms increase of £200 per pupil in this parliament.

Of course, we are still in the first year of the three-year spending review, so only a magician would expect schools to have seen results of the whole three years before the first year is over.

When we were elected, the 1997–8 Budget (which Davies seems to think I was responsible for) had already been agreed and distributed. With Gordon Brown we took immediate action to give schools an emergency injection of £835m extra cash for 1998–9, avoiding a further £40 real-terms cut per pupil.

Nick Davies dismisses increased spending on repairs. Yet twice as much is now being spent as under the Conservatives. With the new deal for schools, over 10,000 schools have already had or are undergoing improvement: much of it substantial. As well as new classrooms for infants and the removal of the last outside toilets, 260 schools are benefiting from substantial buildings improvement or replacement projects through public–private partnerships.

Graciously, Nick Davies concedes that we have increased the standards fund. Yet he has made several errors here too. Few grants rely on bids now. The fund which enables us to provide grants for literacy and numeracy or teacher training has increased from £190m in 1997–8 to over £820m in grant in 2001–2. Some programmes involve 50% (not 60%) match funding from authorities. Others like class sizes and computer funding are funded fully by the government. This is also true from this coming April of the highly popular excellence in cities programme.

Is any of this making a difference? The evidence certainly suggests it is. Standards in the 3Rs have risen as a result of the literacy and numeracy hours. The recent Guardian/ICM poll showed that most primary school parents believe standards in their own primary school had risen as a result. Four times as many primary schools are linked to the Internet and schools are being equipped with computers. Teachers are being trained to use the net.

We are able to fund £2,000 increases in annual pay for good teachers – on top of the annual 3.3% award. Schools in the inner cities have got extra money for mentors to help tackle disaffection as well as new units for disruptive pupils and programmes for able children. I'm acting so that we don't simply leave weak and failing schools to sink as the Tories were happy to do (and as Nick Davies advocated), but at the same time we recognise that good schools should have the chance to flourish without excessive intervention.

We are spending £140m this year on tackling truancy and exclusions compared with £22m a year under the Conservatives. We are spending £160m this year on cutting class sizes – something ignored by the last government.

I know that further and higher education are often relegated to section two of the *Guardian* on a Tuesday, but that is no reason for your star investigator to miss them completely in his lengthy and supposedly comprehensive piece. In fact, further education colleges which educate over 4m students have seen their budgets increase from £3.1bn in 1997–98 to almost £3.9bn in 2001–2. Similarly, extra research funding and more money for standards and access means that universities will get an extra £1bn in spending by 2002, together with £1.4bn for research from the government and Wellcome Trust for research.

Let us imagine two other scenarios. The Liberal Democrats argued for an extra 'penny on income tax' at the last election to fund education. Had they done so, there would have been an extra £2bn a year on top of Conservative spending plans – less than half of what we are spending. Had the Conservatives won the election, we would have had even less funding in real terms than in their last Budget in 1997.

Of course we need to make sure as much of the money as possible gets directly to schools – and I have taken steps to ensure that happens. We need to sustain increased investment in the years to come. The prime minister recognises that as much as I do. But it is as absurd to pretend that what is happening now represents little change from the past as it would be to suggest that we didn't need to see more money for education in the future.

Guardian *readers join the debate*

Here in California the state schools have been destroyed by a similar process to the twenty years of 'free market' politics – with the added evil of racism as a motive for more private education. Without urgent action to redistribute the resources from the rich to pay for the schooling of the poor, British schools could soon be like the battered barracks that pass for children's educational institutions in this state. But, of course, this means taxation along with courageous politicians willing to spell out the reasons for it. There are as few people facing up to that reality in California as there are in Britain.

Paul Cheney
Oakland, USA

Nick Davies is right in his analysis of David Blunkett's confidence trick on education spending. Labour has been fiddling the figures to a staggering extent. A few weeks ago we added up all the re-announcements of money that Labour have made on funding in education. The total came to a staggering £185bn – more than the GDP of Sweden.

They have broken their manifesto commitment to spend a higher proportion of national income on education. House of Commons figures show that education spending as a proportion of GDP is going to be less under Labour than it was under the Conservatives. This is all part of the great Labour lie and proves that they say one thing then do another. Indeed, to match the proportion of GDP spent on education under the last Conservative government, and to honour their manifesto pledge, Labour should be spending an extra £32bn rather than the so-called £19bn on education.

Theresa May MP
Shadow secretary of state for education

Nick Davies writes: 'If you deny the role of social justice in education, you remove any logical justification for universal schooling . . . it makes no economic sense at all.'

There are logical economic justifications. These include higher tax revenues from the higher incomes generated from a better educated working class (empirically evident). Advancements in technology can be utilised more fully by an educated workforce. Education also provides child care that allows working-class parents to work during the day, thus contributing to economic growth. And it makes economic sense from an employer's perspective to recruit the most able and productive workers. Higher education can be used to screen prospective employees, sorting the wheat from the chaff irrespective of social class.

D. Brockton and N. Wrigley
Exeter

The secretary of state's defence was notable for its omissions. Given every opportunity to confirm that spending will be £19bn higher in 2002 than it was in 1998, he failed to do so. I hope the government will never again repeat that now-discredited number.

We are discovering ever more glaring discrepancies between government expenditure plans and spending outcomes. As this Parliament moves into its latter stages, parents, pupils and teachers are entitled to some explanations of the present grim reality, rather than being given more visions of a future that never seems to arrive.

I won't revisit the telling statistics in Nick Davies's article, many of which were based on Liberal Democrat parliamentary questions. But it is a lie that our election pledge would have delivered less than Labour has done. If revenues from 1p on income tax had been added to current spending, £900m more would be invested in education in 2002 than under Labour's plans. If we were to join in Labour's mathematical conjuring we would call it £6.6bn higher – but that's a mistake we do not intend to make.

Phil Willis MP
Lib Dem education spokesman

Nick Davies sheds some light on the obscurities of school funding. In Stockport our ability to deliver anything like the government's headline level of increase has been at the expense of cuts in other council services. Davies exposes some of the myths of the standard spending assessment, but not the discrepancies between LEAs. Parents here find it hard to understand why their children are deemed to be worth £250 a year less than those in apparently comparable boroughs in the south-east.

We will be spending at 3% above SSA. Our pupils deserve better, but there are limits to the sacrifices other services and council tax payers can be asked to make to redress the unfairness of a discredited system. That is why we are part of the Forum for Fairer Education Funding – the grouping of the 40 worst-funded LEAs which hopes to influence the current review of these issues.

Cllr Mark Hunter
Chair of education, Stockport

Here in Haringey education spending had been 'passported' following a critical Ofsted report. This has meant diverting cash from other budgets, and most from social services which suffers total cuts of £3.2m in 2000–1 and £4m in 2001–2. The result is that education for mainstream children is safeguarded while services for vulnerable children with disabilities and in care – not to mention adult disabled and elderly – are made to suffer. The council's social services budgetary strategy is in no doubt that, 'there needs to be an absolute reduction in the level of care provided to existing clients.' This will affect a wide range of children's services such as residential, respite,

rehabilitation and under-fives, and in time generate extra costs and lower standards.
Martin Hewitt
London

Having quashed Nick Davies's concerns about education spending, I trust David Blunkett will now reply to our head teachers' letter wondering why all secondary schools in Northumberland are facing budget cuts next year.
Mark Robson
Morpeth, Northumberland

In rebutting allegations of 'conjuring tricks' David Blunkett compounds his sins: '260 schools are benefiting from substantial building projects through public–private partnership'. That is indeed the aspiration, but in fact only a handful of PFI contracts have been signed and only three new-builds completed. Many are bogged down in the complex procurement process.
Michael Ball
Vice-chair, Pimlico school governors,
London

I was disgusted by the partiality and inaccuracy of the Nick Davies report. I am pleased, therefore that David Blunkett has put the matters straight. Unfortunately, we'll still get letters and articles from clever-Dicks threatening to, or actually leaving, the Labour party. There is no way the damage done to schools over eighteen years of Thatcherism can be put right quickly: only small children expect everything at once.
Ruby Weston
Long Buckby, Northants

THREE

PROBLEMS AND SOLUTIONS

TRUANCY AND EXCLUSION

10 JULY 2000

ONE GOOD THING about spitting is that it helps to pass the time. It's morning, about nine o'clock, and down on the streets of south London the school buses have dumped their loads and the playgrounds have gone quiet. Up here, on the top floor of the tower block, the day has started, as it always does, with Karen and Philly and Annie May and the others sitting slouched on the black-tile floor by the liftshaft, staring at the scorch mark at the top of the rubbish chute, smoking fags, watching the minutes go by and practising their spitting.*

In the past they've tried hanging out in the shopping malls, but the Old Bill hassled them. It's the same on the streets, really. Sometimes, they go round Philly's house – his mum doesn't mind, she's in bed all day. But mostly, each morning they sit here in the block, and if it gets too cold with the wind blowing in from the open walkways they go down on to the estate and, in among the dog crap and the flower tubs filled with fag ends, they find some litter and bring it back up here and light a fire on the landing, and then they sit and watch the smoke. A day in the life of a truant.

It's better than school and, as the morning passes, they sit and sometimes talk, but not too much. When they first started coming up here, they used to play in the lift. It wasn't much of a game: push the button, wait for the lift to arrive, get in,

---

* In order to protect their privacy, the identities of the children in this story have been disguised.

go mental – jump up and down as hard as you can and batter the fuck out of its walls and floor with your feet and your fists – then wait for someone else on another floor to call the lift and hope it doesn't work. There used to be a youth club, near the bottom of the block, but it closed. Down on the ground floor, there's a food store. Annie May says she's seen them picking their noses with their fingers and it's disgusting because then they go back in and touch all the food. She says one of them tried to shag Karen and another girl, and now Karen's got to give evidence on video. She says it's better in summer. They go up the fire escape on to the roof and then they can look down at the streets below and spit on them.

Up here on the block, with half a dozen subdued children, it is easy to imagine that this is a small problem. At first sight, the official statistics confirm this. The Audit Commission says that there are some 12,000 children each year who are permanently excluded from school and a further 150,000 who are excluded temporarily. Which is not ideal, but it is a tiny fraction of the whole pupil population. The commission also says that each year a million of the eight million children in our schools will be absent without authorisation. But many of those absences are for only one day.

The numbers conceal as much as they reveal. They say nothing about the children who are 'cleansed' – pushed out of schools by head teachers who avoid officially recording them as exclusions. They do not mention the children who turn up at school to be registered and then walk straight out. Most of all they ignore all the children who are out of school but who do not qualify to be counted. There is an apparently vast reservoir of students whose absence from school is authorised by parents who want them at home as carers for siblings or who just cannot be bothered to send them. And there are untold thousands who are not registered to any school at all because they have fallen through the system, usually because of their families' unstable lives. Their parents are homeless and shun the authorities for fear of having their kids taken into care; they move and cannot cope with the bureaucracy of a new LEA; they stumble from one sink estate to another, and the education authorities simply lose track of them; they are among the 2,500 children of refugee families who, according to the Refugee Council, are being illegally denied an education; they are the children of travellers; they are in jail.

But this is not about numbers. You really begin to see the scale of the problem only when you first catch a glimpse of what lies beneath it, when you see that the politicians who talk about 'sin bins' and who view this all as a matter of discipline are ignoring or concealing two central truths: first, that the children who spill out of school have bubbled over the edge of a boiling cauldron of trouble, and that this has far less to do with the discipline than it has to do with an epidemic of emotional damage, particularly among the 30% of British children who live in poverty; second, that these children are the most visible part of the central problems of our schools – how to teach the new mass of disaffected children who see no point in learning, how to give any reality at all to the once vibrant idea that education is the natural escape route from poverty. It is a riddle whose solution in this country has been lost and buried in deep-seated structural problems which are being left almost entirely untouched and unchallenged by current government strategy.

Come back to the block. By noon, a few of the faces have pushed off to play on the buses. That's not much of a game either. You get on the bus without a ticket, see how far you can travel before you get thrown off, then you walk home or maybe catch another bus, if you can be bothered. Other faces have arrived now. They all have the same kind of faces, with the shine rubbed off, and the same kind of stories.

Listen to Karen, sitting with her back to the liftshaft wall, listless, aimless, hopeless, the kind of truant who gives David Blunkett nightmares – she's not been to school regularly since she was eleven, and she is now fourteen. Her story is very simple. When she was seven, her father started using heroin and crack cocaine, and fairly soon he got her mother on to it too. Until then, life had been OK. They had a nice house, there was food in the kitchen, she was going to school. Once they started using, the mother and father slid downhill fast, taking Karen and her three younger sisters with them.

Her dad used to take her out thieving. She used to knock on the door, a little girl with gaps in her teeth, and if there was someone in, she'd ask for a glass of water and run along; if not, her dad would smash a window and they'd get inside and take whatever they could. She got arrested for that eventually, when she was eleven, and spent thirty-six hours in a cell. By that time, she had long lost sight of normal life. She says there was no food in the house, and to feed her sisters as well as herself, she'd go and borrow money off friends or eat at someone else's house or nick things from the shops or scavenge in rubbish bins. They had no light in the house, and no heat either. Her mum and dad just did drugs and watched the time go by.

She became the stand-in mother, feeding and caring for the three younger ones. At first, when she stopped going to school, she still took the others, but then it got too much and so they all stopped. From time to time the welfare officer used to come round and bang on the door, and Karen says her mum just told them to blank it and keep quiet and then the welfare officer would go away. If there were letters about it, they just ignored them. Eventually, her dad got sent to jail – four years for robbery – and her mum was left on her own with four children and a heroin habit. And that's the way it still is now.

So why does she not want to sit in school? Because she is too sure there is no point, too scared to be caught out failing, too determined to advertise her indifference, too angry and too cynical – too emotionally damaged. When they are not up here in the block, Karen and the others spend most of their time in some old railway arches which have been converted into a kind of refuge for young people. They are run by a psychotherapist called Camila Batmanghelidjh, who was taken to court by her building society because she stopped paying her mortgage and used the money to set up this day club for the kids under the arches.

Batmanghelidjh reckons that one in three children in the inner cities have some form of emotional or behavioural difficulty. Several hundred children a day find their way to her arches. Most of them are more or less out of school. They live, she says, in a state of 'emotional coldness'. This is the hidden core of what the politicians dismiss as mere truancy and exclusion.

Last year, the Office for National Statistics (ONS) reported that 10% of Britain's children suffer from mental disorders – anxiety, depression, obsessions, clinically significant behaviour disorders and hyperactivity – but that figure (which is worrying enough) masked the real story, which is the concentration of mental disorders among the children of the poor. The ONS found, for example, that among the children of families where both parents are unemployed, some 20% have a mental health problem. They also found that children with this kind of illness were four times more likely to truant than others. They were also three times more likely to have specific learning difficulties, three times more likely to have special educational needs and ten times more likely to be in trouble with the police, all of which findings are linked to the kind of behaviour which leads to children being excluded.

Unhappiness always has its reasons. One of the fourteen-year-old girls who move between the block and Batmanghelidjh's arches has started working from time to time as a street prostitute. It seems she is doing so at the behest of her mother, who needs the money. There is an eleven-year-old boy who lives with his ageing gran because neither of his parents wants anything to do with him; a fifteen-year-old girl whose mother died of cancer years ago, whose father is preoccupied with selling drugs, who has been in and out of care and who had her first abortion at thirteen (she has not been to school for two and a half years); another thirteen-year-old girl who is given money for sex by an elderly man; two brothers, aged seventeen and eleven, both of them drug runners; a twelve-year-old girl who recently found her father after he had overdosed and who has now been sent to live with her mother, who makes no secret of not wanting her. On and on it goes: the fifteen-year-old boy who had been through four prisons and eight children's homes before he was discovered to be suffering from undiagnosed Tourette's Syndrome; the eleven-year-old boy who suffers from severe anxiety and who has just been turfed out of his sixth school.

His nine-year-old sister has a hearing disorder, anxiety attacks and she wets her bed; the two of them live in a room with a concrete floor with a mother who grew up in care, who is said to have no idea how to look after children (she has forbidden them to have any toys). You don't have to diagnose the damage; you can weigh it.

The strategy of the Education Secretary, David Blunkett, is all about 'inclusivity'. He has introduced a complex package of sticks and carrots to persuade schools and LEAs to divert truants and the excluded back into the classroom. By 2002, he wants a reduction of 30% in both statistics; every secondary school and every LEA has been given a target. He is paying new Pupil Support Grants so that a thousand schools can set up Learning Support Units to help them reach the targets. If they miss the targets, he will withdraw their grants. Some schools will also receive money to pay for learning mentors to help disaffected children. He has given LEAs new powers to join appeals against exclusion and made it their responsibility to pick up the bill for the education of those who nevertheless are excluded. Finally, the Home Office has introduced new fines for parents who fail to send their children to school and new powers for police to pick up truants on the streets.

It is important to recognise that this strategy has its merits. Although Mr Blunkett refuses to acknowledge the real importance of poverty, he is targeting extra resources on some of the poorest areas. Funding for learning mentors, for example, is being delivered through the Excellence in Cities programme which is focused on six metropolitan areas. And although the press (including the *Guardian*) constantly describe the new Learning Support Units as 'sin bins' – i.e. places where you throw away bad people – it is a term the DFEE rejects. Behind all the rhetoric about discipline, the reality is that many schools are now attempting to tackle the underlying problems of the most disaffected children.

However, Mr Blunkett's strategy is also riddled with risks, some of them quite alarming. In general, there are two problems. First, the tactics of the new school units and also the DFEE's particular version of mentoring are, at best, untested and, at worst, proven failures. If these schemes fail to change the way in which these children are behaving, we will have locked into our schools a group of the most delinquent and difficult children and we will start to see the kind of violence of student against student, student against teacher, which has become part of the currency of daily life, for example, in some inner-city schools in the United States. Those who nevertheless end up on the streets will find less provision than ever. Mr Blunkett is crossing a precipice on a bridge made of balsa wood.

The second problem – which runs like blood through the DFEE's veins – is that Mr Blunkett's decisions are polluted by politics. In key respects, as we will see, he has, with his left hand, made moves to persuade schools to deal with disaffected children, and then with his right hand, launched politically inspired initiatives which undermine those moves. Beyond that, his strategy suffers, like almost every other step he takes, from his political decision to leave in place the whole package of reforms introduced by the former education secretary, Kenneth Baker, in the late 1980s.

As this series has previously shown, this structure penalises the most disaffected children: they perform badly in exams; their schools tumble down the league tables; middle-class families use their professional skills and their strength in the property market to take their motivated children away to schools with a less disaffected intake; when they move they take funds away with them; the struggling school is left with even fewer motivated children and even less money to educate them, and so it spirals downwards. In short, the children of the poor get the schools with the poorest budgets, an imbalance that is not corrected by the available subsidies for needy children which notoriously are rationed, inefficiently distributed and inadequate in the first place.

Furthermore, these schools have had a direct financial incentive to exclude the most difficult children in order to improve their position in the league tables. As the Baker reforms took hold, exclusions rose fivefold in five years. Leaving Kenneth Baker's system in place, Mr Blunkett has now introduced counter-measures to try to give schools a financial interest in not excluding children. The problem is that neither structure simply provides a neutral framework in which a school can decide a child's future purely on grounds of education and behaviour.

If you visualise class differences in this country as a steep slope, Kenneth Baker came along and built a house which reproduced the whole slope, so that every floor was at a steep angle, tipping the weakest children downwards. David Blunkett bought the house, refused to admit it was crooked, and now runs around nailing the furniture to the floor and yelling at everyone else every time his dinner slides off the table.

More than that, in the specific area of emotional damage, the bad structure goes beyond Kenneth Baker's schooling plans. Come back to the block and to Camila Batmanghelidjh's arches. The morning is past, the afternoon is wearing on and, up in the block, where Batmanghelidjh is not in charge, finally they have found something to do. They are smoking hash. Batmanghelidjh knows they do it. She knows it is part of the daily routine, for as long as they can afford the hash. And worse. She has one twelve-year-old who had rocks of crack cocaine found in his pockets. She has urged them not to do it, but she is not about to hammer them for it, because she knows why it is happening: 'They use cannabis to control their moods.' And why do they do that? Because just about nobody else is doing anything to help them with those moods. The ONS can tell the world that 20% of poor children are mentally ill. Nobody quarrels with the finding (which has been replicated by other studies). But this country's strange and terrible reaction has been to shake its head and then to offer virtually no care at all.

The Audit Commission in 1999 found that less than half the health authorities in the country even had a policy for child mental health and that, among those who did, there were all kinds of gaps and overlaps where different agencies were failing to work together. The ONS similarly, having recorded the scale of mental illness among children, also found that 30% of these children had not been seen even once by a specialist, or even by a GP, let alone been effectively treated. At Young Minds, a national charity working to promote the mental health of children and young people, Deb Loeb told us: 'The waiting lists and lack of resources are just desperate.'

There is a national shortage of child psychiatrists. Four years ago, the NHS executive was recording increasing concern about 'the fragmentation and reduction in child and adolescent mental health services around the country.' This month, the Department of Health told us it has only 180 child psychiatrists in the whole country and that most of those are in the south-east.

There is a national network of educational psychologists, 1,820 of them, but everyone who works in the field says that they have become overwhelmed with the bureaucratic business of assessing children for 'statements' which entitle schools to extra money to help them. Brian Harrison Jennings, secretary of the Association of Educational Psychologists, said: 'We are so busy seeing the next child being referred to us that we don't have time to implement the very course of action that we recognise they would benefit from. All we can do is to refer them to someone else and, for the most part, that someone else may not be able to see them either.' A south London parent whose school has 115 children with special educational needs, of whom only one has so far been statemented, told us: 'Round here, educational psychologists come round about as often as Halley's Comet.'

The 'statementing' of children has itself become part of the problem, subverted by spending cuts and overwhelmed by demand. The Audit Commission last year found that only 48% of draft statements are prepared within the statutory timescale of eighteen weeks; one in ten trusts could not offer an appointment within six months of referral; and in five areas, the average wait for an assessment was more than a year. Even if the child is assessed, its appeal for money goes to the local Special Needs Panel, whose funds have been so rationed that frequently they will cover only a minimal number of hours' support in the school. Baroness Warnock, whose 1978 inquiry introduced statementing, now regards the system as a disaster. (Mr Blunkett might note that in the *TES* in December 1999 she said it was 'strikingly absurd' that her inquiry had been forbidden to count social deprivation as in any way contributing to educational needs.) In June 2000, the government withdrew plans for a new bill which was intended to reorganise the whole area of special educational needs.

The only other specialist support for disaffected children comes from educational welfare officers (EWOs). Like the educational psychologists, they have become overwhelmed, each of them responsible for an average of three thousand children, according to the National Foundation for Educational Research, who found EWOs were frequently too busy with the paperwork of truancy even to begin to deal with its causes.

For the most part, the damaged children are left with their parents, who often are part of the problem, and with their teachers, who have very little time and even less specialist training. Researchers from the National Association of Social Workers in Education recorded in a 1998 report the voice of a single damaged child who spoke for the thousands: 'I was having troubles at home, I was having troubles in the school, and the troubles that were in school were coming home and I wouldn't say nothing to the school because I didn't want any more trouble.'

It is easy to imagine that there is a safety net somewhere else, that the children outside the liftshaft in the block are unusual. They are not. All over the country, we found children out of school whose lives are grossly disfigured and who were receiving no effective help: an eleven-year-old girl in Kent who was spending her evenings in a van while her mother, a prostitute, pleasured punters in the back (no school for eighteen months when we last heard of her); a fourteen-year-old girl in Hammersmith who had been living in a car with her homeless parents; an eleven-year-old boy, also in Hammersmith, who was found abandoned at Heathrow Airport; a diaspora of Somalian children, some of whom have seen their parents killed; a fifteen-year-old girl in North Wales who was sleeping on a bench outside the local social services office and still could not get help.

Now look again at David Blunkett's strategy for truancy and

exclusion. The whole structure rests on the effectiveness of the various in-school projects which will attempt to cope with these damaged children. If they fail, the whole thing collapses in disarray and disorder. The biggest scheme – and the only one which is being nationally coordinated – is the introduction of mentors as guides and role models for difficult children.

The idea comes from the United States, where researchers have found that the Big Brothers Big Sisters movement has had real success, but the same researchers warned that 'these findings do not mean that the benefits of mentoring occur automatically'. Although the DFEE has quoted this research in support of its scheme, it has failed so far to introduce the kind of rigorous screening of volunteers, training, supervision and support on which the American scheme relies. When the DFEE commissioned its own research from the Centre for Social Action (CSA), the result was a loud alarm bell.

Echoing the warning from the United States, the CSA reported that 'mentoring is not a panacea that will magically cut crime long-term, reduce exclusion and reduce youth unemployment at a stroke'. It warned that the DFEE needed to invest heavily, and when it looked at one project in detail, it found signs that the DFEE had failed to create effective schemes on the American model: 'The mentoring relationships created are too shallow to make a difference and only have value to the young person as a means of avoiding lessons and the opportunity of a free trip.' The CSA concluded: 'What is regrettable is seeing the potential of this form of practice wasted through insufficient planning, lack of money, lack of communication and lack of a philosophical base that values young people's participation.'

And yet, the schools minister, Estelle Morris, in May 2000, claimed that there was already evidence that the DFEE mentoring was having 'a positive impact on pupils' behaviour, attendance at school and attitudes to learning'. Her department made no mention of the CSA findings but said that the minister was referring to evidence which had been produced by the National Foundation for Educational Research. We checked. In fact, the NFER report produced no statistical evidence whatsoever of any improvement in attendance or any other aspect of pupil behaviour. Oddly, the NFER researchers decided not to interview any of the children involved, nor to use questionnaires which some of them completed. Instead, they quoted positive anecdotal comments from some of the organisers and then revealed without comment the startling fact that the average time that children spent with their mentors was only one hour a fortnight during the academic year, i.e. twenty-one hours in a calendar year. Set this beside the conclusion of the US researchers who studied schemes where children were spending 120 hours over fifteen months with their mentors and concluded: 'The time together does not seem sufficient to offset poor school performance, negative influences on self-esteem and fourteen or more years of living in poverty. While mentors can teach responsibility and values, discuss the importance of education and trying one's best, they cannot be expected to completely neutralise the harsh conditions in which many of these adolescents live.' Estelle Morris added: 'The results under my department's programmes speak for themselves.'

So far as the myriad different in-school projects are concerned, there is simply no evidence at all of whether they will succeed or fail. Clearly, they are well intentioned, and although some are simply exercises in policing to catch truants and bring them back to school, others are imaginative efforts to tackle children's problems: Circles of Friends, where schools use the peer pressure of successful students; Behaviour Support Teams, which pass behaviour-management techniques on to teachers, support staff and parents; Nurture Groups, which separate difficult children and attempt to teach them how to be students. Some schools are reporting encouraging signs of progress.

However, almost all of these schemes suffer from a potentially devastating weakness. They rely on the same over-stretched network of specialists who are already struggling to find time to work effectively, and so they attempt to delegate skills to teachers and parents and others, none of whom has any specialist training at all. As a result, they cannot be and do not claim to be therapeutic in any meaningful sense. Teachers are not therapists.

Mr Blunkett's strategy leaves the gaping void in the care of emotionally damaged children quite unfilled. There are a few genuinely therapeutic schemes in schools. The Place To Be, for example, sends trained counsellors into twenty-eight schools in the London area and is supported by the DFEE. And there are private schemes, like Camila Batmanghelidjh's arches, which struggle to survive without any statutory funding from the DFEE or anyone else. The rest is at best a shot in the dark and at worst a shot in the head for school staff.

If the approach to disaffected children is frail, the approach to disaffected parents is even weaker. Jenny Price, of the Association for Education Welfare Managers, told us: 'Fewer truant in the traditional sense, i.e. absenteeism without people knowing. What is more common is parents who don't care if they go to school or not, or allow them to stay at home to look after the house or after the kids. There is more of that, and it is more difficult to deal with.' In a sweep on the streets of Sheffield last month, officials found 200 children who should have been in school, 75% of whom were absent with 'flimsy excuses' from parents. (One family suggested it was the only convenient time when they could buy a hamster.) EWOs say that where once, any absence at all would have been investigated, now a parent who writes letters can keep their child off school without much fear of being investigated. If they do get a visit, we were told, all they need to do is to hide behind the door: the EWO is going to be too busy to come back very often, particularly when they have un-authorised absences to deal with.

To deal with these parents, the DFEE is relying on heavier fines and the new home–school contracts which were introduced last year at a cost of £1.6 million with clear political benefits but without any obvious impact at all on the problem parents. We met truant parents who had been sleeping with their children in a playground, who had fled their homes under siege from violent neighbours, who were addicted to drugs or alcohol or crushed by depression, or who complained bitterly that their children were too terrified of gang-bullying to go anywhere near their school. When we asked them about the effect of the new fines and the home–school contracts, they just shrugged.

This profoundly fragile structure has then been undermined by decisions which appear to be political rather than educational. The Social Exclusion Unit (SEU) and the Audit Commission both studied truancy and exclusion and both stressed that government strategy must be 'joined up', involving all of the different local agencies that might be able to help. In October 1998, David Blunkett adopted this view and asked LEAs to prepare three-year plans involving all their agencies, to take effect in April 1999. However, in July 1999, just as his officials had finished approving all the plans, he changed his mind and, as part of his political drive to divert power and money away from the LEAs, he announced that schools would have to take over the job. He gave them only six weeks over the summer holidays to comment on his change of direction.

This devolution not only caused short-term chaos but posed a long-term threat to the idea of a 'joined-up' approach by putting all of the other agencies in a secondary position, relying on schools to come to them with money, instead of being a directly funded part of an LEA plan. The Local Government Association (LGA) has warned education ministers that their inclusion strategy has been 'seriously jeopardised by compulsory devolution'. SEU officials also are said to have complained bitterly. Mr Blunkett has been unmoved.

One particularly worrying part of this devolution has been the attempt to make EWOs work for schools instead of their LEAs. Can EWOs criticise schools which are also their employers? What cover will there be if the EWO is off sick? How can an EWO work effectively with a family whose children are separated in different schools, or maintain a link with a child who moves school within the area? The LGA complains that 'policies have been adopted wholesale before they have been evaluated'. The move contradicted advice from the Audit Commission who favoured a central organisation. Under pressure, the DFEE has agreed that it will review the policy after a one-year pilot.

Mr Blunkett launched a further political initiative which

also threatens to damage the chances of success for his in-school units – Performance-Related Pay for teachers. The object of all these units is to work with difficult children and then to reintegrate them back into the classroom as soon as possible and, at the very latest, according to Mr Blunkett's guidelines, within two terms. The history of units for difficult children, in or out of school, is dominated by the difficulty of this kind of reintegration.

We spoke to a specialist educational social worker who had worked in a successful therapeutic unit in the past. She told us: 'You can build up wonderful relationships with the kids, that's the good side of it, but you can't integrate them back into the system. I worked for two or three months with this boy to get him to a point where he would go back to school. He arrives on the first morning and after two minutes some teacher pulls him up and says, "Where's your tie? Go back home and get your tie." And it all falls apart. And all I can say to the teacher is "Fuck you." I mean it. That is what I said.'

The new deal on performance-related pay will give experienced teachers a bonus of £2,000, but only if, among other things, their results improve. This adds a new financial incentive to reject the reintegration of a student who is likely to perform badly and to disrupt the class. The result is that at the same time as he is trying to negate the school's incentive to exclude difficult children, Mr Blunkett has introduced a new incentive for teachers to do precisely the opposite of what he wants. The upshot is that, on the ground, a crooked extension is being built on the side of the crooked house.

You have to understand that the DFEE's new investment disguises a simultaneous cut in the education of disaffected children. For years, truants and the excluded have been offered a safety net of 320 LEA Pupil Referral Units (PRUs) outside schools. This network is notoriously inadequate, catering for only a fraction of the needy children, with some eight thousand places for the tens of thousands who might need them. There has been nothing unusual in a child waiting a year between a permanent exclusion and a place in a PRU. When finally it comes, it often involves only a few hours of teaching each week, usually in an inadequate building and without any kind of specialist resources to tackle the child's problem. One PRU teacher told us: 'They tell us we have to teach them *Macbeth* and we say "But they can't read", so they say "Well, play them the video."' Now, this safety net is to be cut.

In Mr Blunkett's plan, LEAs no longer have a statutory responsibility for truants outside school. Pregnant schoolgirls and young mothers similarly will be dropped by the PRUs. If they choose to, LEAs are now free to make substantial savings by simply closing any out-of-school unit that was helping truants or schoolgirl mothers. They must continue to provide for any student who is excluded for more than three weeks – but many are cutting back even these units, on the assumption that all of their schools will succeed in hitting their targets for retaining these pupils within school walls.

According to LEA documents, Sheffield, for example, will now provide only 'the minimum necessary for compliance with statutory duties'. This means: getting rid of 16% of its PRU teachers; completely closing the two units which deal with truants; closing the unit for pregnant girls; then reducing the time available in units for the excluded. The remaining out-of-school units will provide limited short-term help for excluded secondary children ('The aim of the LEA is that all excluded children below Key Stage Four will be reintegrated into school.') and nothing at all for excluded primary children ('The target for primary-aged pupils is that they . . . will not be excluded.'). The provision of regular therapeutic care in these units will continue at its present level: i.e. there will be none.

Alongside these reduced PRUs, Sheffield is providing learning mentors in every secondary school, new Learning Support Units in nine of them, and a Pupil Inclusion Team to track pupils and offer advice to schools. This is an improvement in one sense: in-school places are cheaper and they are being subsidised by the DFEE, and so the in-school units can cater for more children than the old PRUs. But the whole strategy relies on one thing – that the schools will hit their targets and succeed in keeping the children within their walls ('The reorganisation of the PRUs reflects those targets.') The

LEA documents admit that this will be tough: 'It will be difficult to foresee exactly what remaining central needs will be, as the task of inclusion is extremely challenging.' In addition to the cut in the national PRUs, children are being gradually shifted out of the 1,148 special schools and into the mainstream.

The key question for the future is: What happens if the schools miss their targets? What happens if – under the cumulative strain of the profound shortage of effective therapy, the weakening of the 'joined-up' strategy, the reverse incentives of league tables and now performance-related pay – the entire balsa-wood bridge starts to collapse? If the truants still walk out of the school gates and find nothing, if the excluded are still pushed out of the gates and find even less of a safety net than there used to be, more and more of them will end up on the streets: more child crime, more prostitution, more street gangs, more aimless, listless, hopeless kids on tower-block landings.

On paper, the DFEE have an answer to this: schools will hand over their Pupil Support Grant to the LEA, who will then make provision. In practice, however, LEA officials warn that schools are going to be very reluctant to hand over much needed cash and, even if they do, LEAs will no longer have the PRUs to deal with the children.

And what will be happening within the schools? If the in-school units do not succeed in rapidly recycling disaffected children back into the classroom, they will fill up and impose a strict gate-keeping policy. Only the most disaffected children will be able to use them, making it particularly difficult for staff to succeed with them. Back in the classroom, teachers will wrestle with those who should be in the units but cannot find a place. For some children, the new system actually provides an incentive to rebel: if they know they cannot be excluded, they may be tempted to be even more disruptive; if they know that there is no unit to scoop them up outside if they play truant, they may be even more likely to walk out of the gate. And this is only the first phase. Remember that if any schools fail to hit their targets for cutting truancy and exclusion, the DFEE will withdraw the new money it is giving them. They will hit a downward spiral.

And there is no mystery about which schools are most likely to slide down that spiral. It will not be the middle-class schools with their well-motivated intake, it will be the struggling ones, those overburdened with difficult pupils and who are already suffering the financial penalties of Kenneth Baker's reforms. Down they will go again, with the DFEE pushing their heads under the water like a swimming-pool bully.

We do not have to guess what this could mean. LEAs and governing bodies are already reacting to Mr Blunkett's package of sticks and carrots by fighting head teachers who try to exclude difficult pupils; LEAs are pressurising some schools by warning that their exclusions might be challenged in court and that the LEAs would not support the school's legal costs. The future is already happening. One of the teacher unions, the NAS/UWT, which has been campaigning against the DFEE's strategy, compiled a list of incidents in the first four months of this year, where teachers had been ordered to teach children who would otherwise have been excluded. A sample: 'Cumbria: 13-year-old boy, last year indecently assaulted welfare assistant, excluded but returned on appeal because of "procedural errors", now boy indecently assaults girl pupil in PE lesson . . . Lincolnshire: 14-year-old boy, reinstated by appeal panel after permanent exclusion following repeated instances of verbal and sexual abuse of women staff . . . Oxfordshire: 14-year-old boy, permanent exclusion following three violent incidents including assault of deputy head, parents appeal, appeal allowed on procedural grounds . . . Greater London: 14-year-old boy, history of violent conduct, elbowed teacher in stomach, permanently excluded, LEA overturned exclusion . . . Rhondda: 15-year-old girl, history of substance abuse and violence to other pupils, threatened woman teacher, permanent exclusion overturned by Governors advised by LEA . . . Hertfordshire: 10-year-old boy, history of violence and disruption, attacked another pupil and woman teacher who intervened, head reluctant to exclude fearing might be

148

overruled by LEA . . . Tyneside: 15-year-old boy, excluded from previous school for violent behaviour, attacked teacher with screwdriver, head reluctant to exclude permanently . . .'

The NAS/UWT is warning not just that these incidents are occurring but that they are increasing in frequency. So far, this country has seen only one head teacher killed by his students; we don't have firearms in our schools, but we do have knives; gang fights are relatively rare, but we do have assaults and extortion; rapes are rare, but sexual harassment in the playground is not; drug syndicates are rare, but drugs are not. All this is sitting out there, waiting for us.

THE BIG CHEAT – THE PROBLEM
WITH RISING STANDARDS

11 JULY 2000

THERE WERE EIGHTEEN children in a classroom. All of them had three things in common: they were all studying *Macbeth* for GCSE English; they had all turned in essays to be assessed as part of their GCSE; and not one of them had written a single word of any of the essays, because their teacher (with a little help from her husband) had spent the weekend writing the whole lot for them.

This teacher says that routinely she writes her students' coursework and that a lot of her colleagues do the same. 'I do it for two reasons. First, you give the kid a chance, and second, you don't get beaten over the head. Otherwise you get the blame for the fact that the kids don't do any work, or don't even turn up, and for the fact that the national curriculum is crap and doesn't do anything for a load of kids. You are bullied. The bullying of staff by senior management in schools is appalling.'

Welcome to the other side of David Blunkett's drive for higher standards, to the world of tests and targets, where the career prospects of a teacher or the future of a whole school can be wrecked by one bad set of statistics, a world where teachers have been taught to fear failure with such an intensity that they have learned to cut corners to survive. Welcome to the Big Cheat.

We have spoken to teachers, head teachers, LEA advisers, Ofsted inspectors, officials and leaders of teacher unions, and we have not found a single one of them who has not heard of some kind of cheating to deliver the figures which the

150

Secretary of State now requires. The cheating which they report goes far beyond GCSE course work – to multiple fiddles on SATs tests and GCSEs, the wholesale fabrication of figures on truancy and attendance, the falsification of records on excluded children. It is certain that not all teachers have been driven to cheat; equally, our evidence suggests that the fiddling is now widespread.

The significance of the Big Cheat is not simply that Mr Blunkett's figures are infected with fiction. Beneath the fiddling, there is little doubt that in the last ten years there has been some real advance in the standards achieved in Britain's state schools. The more important point is that it is yet another sign of the enduring weakness of New Labour's attack on poor standards, that their underlying analysis of failure is mistaken, with the result that their strategy repeatedly evades the real problems and imposes the entire burden of change on teachers and managers.

As we have seen, the most important single factor in a school's failure to hit academic targets is its intake of children, and in particular of the 30% of Britain's children who live with the damaging effects of poverty. The government swats this aside with its mantra that 'poverty is no excuse' and persists with Kenneth Baker's market in school places, even though it penalises the schools with the most impoverished intake. Beyond that, school failure reflects financial limits – large classes, scarce equipment, poor buildings, stressed teachers. As we have shown, New Labour has lied grossly about the amount of extra money which it is investing in schools. Failing effectively to tackle these underlying problems, the government has inflicted overwhelming pressure on teachers and managers to deliver all of the necessary change themselves. There is no doubt that there was room for teachers and managers to improve – but they alone cannot deliver a change on the scale demanded. And so, some of those who have the most difficult intakes of children and/or the most stifling financial problems have learned to cheat to survive.

In order to make it harder for the Department for Education to blame individuals instead of acknowledging its own core strategy as the cause of the problem, we have disguised the identity of almost all of those who spoke to us. As one West Country teacher put it: 'The emperor has no clothes. We all know the system is ridiculous but we don't do anything about it. It's just a game we play.' Or, to be precise, a collection of games.

Take, for example, the Truancy Game. The object is to make your attendance figures look good. This has been important since the mid-1990s, when Ofsted started to log attendance as an indicator of a school's progress and the DFEE started to publish annual figures. Now it has become an even higher priority: David Blunkett has announced that by the year 2002, schools must reduce the number of days lost to truancy by 30%. Schools who fail to hit their targets are liable to lose funds.

The Truancy Game is played on a desk top. Points are scored by obliterating the evidence of unauthorised absences, and players can score these points in two simple ways: by pretending that an absent child was really in the school, or by admitting that the child was absent but pretending that there was a legitimate reason. Although the rules are simple, experienced players have developed different tactics.

There are some who like to wait for the end of term and then spend a whole day on the figures, like this senior teacher at a secondary school in an inner-city area: 'At the end of term, if you've got less than, say, 92%, which is your attendance target, then you go right back through the register and you start putting in "present". You can do it with the new electronic registers just the same. Sometimes it's the head who says to the person who's doing the returns, to work on the figures, sort of "We need our attendance at such and such, so make sure we get there."

'It's a lot of work, you have to write in loads of "presents". You think about it: if you've been doing two registers a day, it comes to about 150,000 attendances in one term, and if you find out you've only got 87% and you need 92 or 93%, you've got to put in about 7,000 extra "presents" – all those new "present" marks you've got to put in. It takes ages. And, if you're sensible, you have to think about it a bit. You can't go on doing it with the kids who are truanting all the time; you might get the social worker investigating and it'll bugger up all the evidence.'

Other players prefer to keep the ball rolling all through the term, with a little fiddling each day, usually by pretending that somebody like a parent or a doctor has authorised a child to be absent, as numerous teachers explained: 'You just write "letter sent" or "letter received", or it could have been a phone call . . . You can use religious holidays . . . No one checks, you just say the absence was authorised.' Other fiddles are opportunistic. 'We had to close the school for the day, because the heating broke down, so we put it down as 100% attendance . . . We have children in the behaviour unit who often only get taught for half the day, but it gets put down as a whole day.'

The game is so widespread that it is scarcely secret at all. Here is a former head teacher, now a nationally respected expert on the improvement of schools: 'I know that schools have fixed the attendance figures and I believe the government cannot be unaware of it.' Or here is one of Ofsted's registered inspectors, formerly a senior LEA official: 'Fiddling attendance figures is dead common. It's easy.' Or this school clerk from the East Midlands: 'We fiddle them because we have absolutely no control over how many children come to school.' Or the deputy head from east London: 'I don't feel any shame about it at all. There is no other way to do it. And that's the truth. Everybody does it.'

For those who prefer something with a little more skill and imagination, the government has also organised the Great Exclusion Game, an exercise in vanishing acts. Just as with truancy, Mr Blunkett has set a target for the number of excluded children to be cut by 30% by 2002 with the threat of financial penalties for those who fail. So the trick here is to exclude children without admitting it. When you talk to the players, you find there is really not that much skill involved.

'It's "jump before you're pushed". You get hold of the parent and you say: "If you leave him here, we're going to have to kick him out, it'll be on his record for ever and he'll never get a job, so why don't you take him out yourself before it happens?" It usually works.' Some head teachers call this 'cleansing': hardly anyone admits that they are doing it, but just about everybody knows someone else who has. Jenny Price of the Association for Education Welfare Managers told us: 'Children whose faces don't fit, children who will never get the required number of A to C grades or whose behaviour is disruptive: these children are removed off rolls. You cannot believe how easy it is. Nobody follows it up, nobody chases it.'

It is, in fact, the oldest trick in the current Big Cheat book, and officials in the Department of Education and the Social Exclusion Unit admit that it has been happening. A few players show signs of real ingenuity, like Firfield School in Newcastle, which was caught out by *Channel 4 News* in 1999 arranging for the parents of regular truants to sign letters offering to educate their children at home. The parents had no such intention and said they signed the letters simply because they were told to. Never mind. It took the children off the school roll without chalking up any exclusions, so it made the figures look better. Which is what it's all about.

A temporary exclusion is just as easy and, by all accounts, just as widespread: 'You just phone the parents up and say: "We're sending him home and we don't want him back till Tuesday." They just accept it. It's usually because there's been some pretty bad incident, so they're not going to argue about it. We don't log it as an exclusion, so it doesn't count as one. The only problem is that if we want to go for a forty-five-day exclusion, we can't do it, because we haven't recorded all the others.' As a variation, children are told to come in for half-days only.

The pressure to deliver statistical ends without genuine means now runs through the system. The *Guardian* last year reported that there was widespread evidence of schools cheating during Ofsted tests: renting expensive IT equipment for the duration of the inspection, hiding disruptive pupils, fiddling class records, making weak teachers take time off and temporarily replacing them with supply staff. We have been told of schools who helped themselves out of special measures by using LEA advisers to stand in for teachers who were likely to be criticised by visiting HM inspectors.

There is no doubt that the most demanding play is seen in the Exam Games. SATs tests have become a central part of school life, the raw material for the league tables which, despite widespread acknowledgement of their failure to tell the truth about schools, have become firmly lodged as the key indicator of a school's success with critical implications for future enrolment and funding. The pressure from the DFEE has been intense since the Secretary of State announced that he would resign if by 2002 he could not get 80% of eleven-year-olds to reach Level Four in English and 75% of them in maths. Chief officers at local education authorities say that Mr Blunkett's officials agreed to local SATs targets but then found that the national total was too low for the Secretary of State and went back to some LEAs and imposed new higher targets which they believe are quite unrealistic.

There is almost no pattern to the play in SATs tests, more like an orgy of improvisation as different teachers slip through different loopholes in search of ways to meet the pressure. Some of the loopholes are more or less legitimate, encouraged even: extra classes to prepare children for the tests; practice on last year's papers, which are being sold in increasing quantities; the teaching of specific test-related skills, such as the lay out and style for writing a letter, which is a regular question in English tests. The DFEE says much of this is simply part of improving literacy and numeracy, and they supply £42 million for 'booster classes' for children approaching SATs. However, in a narrow distinction, they also say that they do not recommend 'cramming or teaching to the test', and there are many teachers who say that this whole focus on SATs is a perversion of education.

Some of the loopholes are more controversial, albeit they fall short of outright cheating: teachers who tell children that SATs are 'the most important exams you'll ever take' and that their future sets will depend on them; the head teacher who wanders around the exam room, suggesting: 'You might want to have another look at that answer'; the invigilator who knows his students are answering a question about the essential conditions of life and who is asked how to spell 'carbon dioxide', and who replies for the whole class to hear 'You don't need to know how to spell carbon dioxide'; the English teacher who supplies half a dozen 'wizard words' – sophisticated, unusual words – for the children to memorise so they can scatter them throughout their English answers to impress the markers; invigilators who ignore the clock and let children have as much time as they want to complete their test.

And then there are the loopholes which everyone knows amount to cheating. We spoke to some of those who mark SATs tests and who see the clues in the answers: the school where every single child used almost exactly the same form of words to describe how shadows are made; the incorrect answers crossed out and replaced with correct ones; the school whose children reproduced the wording from an official answer sheet; the papers where tick-boxes are filled out in a hand that is stronger and neater than that on the written parts of the paper. The markers say they are supposed to report evidence of malpractice. They all said they didn't: too much hassle; their own marking would then have to be checked; they felt some solidarity with the classroom teachers. Some said they had made reports but that their anxieties had been dismissed.

Then we spoke to teachers and head teachers who explained how it is done. Some of them talked about how easy it was to make changes to children's answers, particularly if they wrote in pencil or if you arranged for all of them to share a batch of brand-new pens; and about how it was almost impossible to be a helper, when you can quite legitimately explain the question to children, without also beginning to explain the answer. An Ofsted inspector, who is also a private consultant and had dropped into a school to pick up some documents, told us he had found the teachers simply writing the answers to the SATs test on the board. 'And this was a convent,' he said. 'These were nuns cheating.'

But most of all, they talked about the Main Trick, the numerous different ways in which teachers can get an early sight of the test papers. This turns out to be rather simple. Eighty per cent of the eleven thousand SATs tests markers are teachers, and in order to standardise the marking, the examination boards have to give them access to the papers ten days before the exam. In the same way, the exam boards also employ a further 1,100 teachers as team leaders who tour the country lecturing markers and who get to see the papers twenty-four days before they are officially revealed; others work as consultants who help the Qualifications and Curriculum Agency (QCA) to set the papers and who know the rough contents of the papers some twelve months before the children sit them.

The QCA and the DFEE both told us emphatically that this causes no problem. There is no system for checking the behaviour of markers, team leaders or consultants. 'We don't see this as a loophole,' a QCA spokesman said. The teachers who see the advance papers beg to differ. Some said simply that it took a will of iron to say nothing to their colleagues or to their students; others admitted priming their pupils and some that they had applied for these positions precisely so that they would be able to get early sight of the papers and prepare their children accordingly. At the conference of the National Union of Teachers in April this year, there was open talk in the bars about the (supposedly secret) contents of the papers to be set in May. We were told, for example: 'Everyone's been told the Key Stage Two children have to know all about walls – Vietnam Wall, Great Wall of China, and so on. Apparently, there's a whole section on that.' Sure enough, the English SATs paper which was unveiled in mid-May included a section where children had to absorb and reproduce information about famous walls, Vietnam, China, etc.

Armed with this information, teachers can simply prime their children, or even persuade them to memorise set answers. A school governor in Yorkshire wrote to us that his head teacher had 'heard stories about schools teaching pupils the answers to the actual questions; schools that put up the answers on classroom walls in the guise of educational aids; schools where teachers check papers as they are being written and make sure that answers are correct before they are handed in.'

157

It does not always work, as a senior teacher in London explained: 'I was teaching Key Stage Three English, we were doing *Romeo and Juliet*, and I had very low-ability kids. We got the question in advance, I can't remember how, but anyway I wrote out the answer and I said to them: "Just take it home and learn it, all right?" Which was OK, and then when it came to the paper, two of them went and did the question on *Twelfth Night*.'

Beyond this, every head teacher in the country is sent the SATs papers a week or ten days before their students are due to sit them. Head teachers told us there was little chance of being caught if they did open papers in advance. 'And if you do open them and have a read, all you need to close them up is a heat-sealer, which is quite a common piece of equipment in a school.'

Barry Dawson, chair of the National Primary Headteachers Association, which supports the use of SATs tests but opposes league tables, said: 'Heads and teachers are under such pressure that inevitably some will be tempted to bend the rules, and the current system is not rigorous enough to stop this. There is not anything like a rigorous system to check whether the tests have been opened or whether the tests are administered fairly.'

LEAs carry out spot checks to make sure that the papers are not opened in advance, and the DFEE told us that 'the incidence of the QCA finding anything untoward is so low as to be inexpressible'. However, the LEAs are short of inspectors, and the QCA acknowledges that the reality is that 90% of schools receive no spot check when they sit SATs. Heads have to sign a declaration that they will keep the SATs papers secure, but there is no set punishment for a head who is caught out, and the QCA has dealt with cases where the LEA decided to take no action against heads who broke the declaration.

A head teacher in Sheffield was suspended after a colleague accused her of 'irregularities in the administration of SATs exams'. Another in Essex felt so guilty after talking to pupils about the contents of the papers they were to sit, that he reported himself to the chair of governors and resigned. In

Devon, a head teacher resigned last year after being accused by a colleague of similar behaviour (although the LEA there has done its best to conceal the incident). The *Guardian* does not know how many other heads have given in to temptation. Nor does the DFEE.

Just as with the truancy game, there is a strong suspicion that this is an open secret. An HM inspector who retired last year after some twenty years in the job said he had seen 'ridiculous and dishonest pursuits' to improve SATs results. An Ofsted registered inspector said: 'Secondary heads usually know which primary heads are fiddling because the children arrive and cannot work to the level of their SATs results. Fiddling at Key Stage Two is probably pretty widespread. The policing is very weak.' His view is echoed by a retired secondary school head, who acknowledged that heads can open SATs papers: 'There would be nothing to stop a head teacher preparing the children for the test.'

The difficulty is that fiddling is contagious, like steroids among athletes: if one teacher does well by cheating, the straight teacher looks worse than ever and is under more pressure than ever to conform to the new line. Under relentless pressure from the Home Office, the police have suffered a similar epidemic, as the *Guardian* and Channel 4's *Dispatches* disclosed in 1999, when only four of the forty-three forces in the country were not fabricating figures for reported crime and for detections, some of them on a massive scale: the pressure to compete with other forces who fiddle and flourish is almost irresistible.

GCSEs are better policed than SATs, and the evidence is that cheating by teachers is less common. Nevertheless, it happens. We found secondary school teachers who are routinely writing the course work which counts towards their students' GCSE results. If there are drawings to do, they produce them, and the children stencil or copy them; if there are essays, the teachers produce them and either print them up with different typefaces or ask children to write them out in longhand. 'Some of them know why I'm asking them to write things out. With some of them, I just say: "Can you do me a favour? Write this out, I want to put it on the wall."'

Teachers put long hours into doing their students' work for them: 'I taught GNVQ business and admin to eleven kids, the average attendance for the class was 63%. I'm between a rock and a hard place. If I don't do the course work, I'm going to get zero passes. And no one is going to say: "Oh, that's understandable." So I did everything I could, I bit the bullet. They had to do three different elements with three different modules: I was creating itineraries for them, I made up interviews they had done with people in business, wrote letters they were supposed to have sent to businesses, everything I could.'

And there are some subtle manipulations. A recently retired secondary head told us: 'If you are clever, you can improve your GCSE results by picking the right exam board for the right subjects. There are different pass rates and you can make quite a difference to your outcomes without making any difference at all to the children's education.' Apparently on the same logic, more schools are taking drama GCSEs because they are said to be easy route to an A to C grade; and some are dropping German and Spanish as their second modern language and starting to teach Mandarin Chinese as an easier grade-scoring option.

Although there is a stronger tradition of security around GCSEs than around SATs, it appears to be breaking down. This is partly because, unlike earlier times, schools now have a conflict of interest, since it is their performance as well as that of their students which is being tested and also, teachers claim, because the exam boards, which are now privatised bodies, have no commercial interest in proper policing. A regular invigilator said he had never yet seen a board inspector visit an exam in progress. Another teacher described how on one occasion neither she nor her students had been able to produce some practical course work: 'The exam moderator came in to look at it, so we kept making excuses, we told him we'd get him the work in a minute, and in the end, he just signed the sheet to say he'd seen the work, but it didn't exist. What does he care? These exam boards are businesses. They don't want to go making a school's life difficult. He just went off home.'

As a safety net for those who cannot deliver the right exam figures, there is also some evidence of schools looking for mitigation by misrecording their base figures, particularly the 'prior attainment' levels of incoming pupils and the number of children who are poor enough to qualify for free school meals. A north London teacher told us: 'My head teacher certainly exaggerates the FSM figures to make the exam results look better. As long as a child has been entitled to claim FSM once in the past, it can continue to do so in the future. You never come off the list. There is no monitoring afterwards. The paperwork is really sloppy.'

The DFEE and QCA both assured us that there was no problem with the exam results, producing the unusual circumstances of a cacophony of confessors all admitting their 'crimes' while the police insist that they are innocent. This may reflect the further new conflict of interest, that these exams now test not only the schools as well as the students, but also the performance of the DFEE, whose Secretary of State has staked his career on raising standards.

Generally, these are the most curious of games: a mass spectator sport with the odd exception that the spectators – the parents and the taxpayers – don't understand what is happening; games played with enormous determination, with the even odder exception that the players cannot win. If the figures are bad, the players will get the blame and may lose their jobs; if the figures are good, however, the Secretary of State steps forward to take the prize.

Finally, there is conflicting evidence on whether the government is not merely enjoying the results of this cheating but actively stimulating it by making exams less demanding. James Sabben-Clare, the head of Winchester College, told last year's conference of head teachers that he had no doubt that, despite government denials, A levels had become easier. Statisticians have queried last year's improvement in Key Stage Two results which, they say, is so uniformly consistent across every part of the country as to invite the suspicion that the threshold marks were lowered. GCSE improvements, they say, look far more genuine, since they vary from area to area.

SATs markers have some worrying stories about

instructions which they say they have been given by team leaders appointed by the QCA to conduct one-day training sessions. In one example, a group of experienced markers all agreed that a test paper should be given a Level Three, below the expected standard for eleven-year-olds. The team leader reportedly seemed embarrassed and suggested that if they looked more carefully, they might like to agree it was a Level Four. 'You're joking,' replied the veteran markers. The team leader tried to insist, provoking the most cynical of the markers to say: 'Oh, so David Blunkett gets to keep his job, does he?'

The same group of markers report that they were told that when children were asked in their English SATs tests to list in order the dates when famous walls were built, they could pass if they got the dates right, even if they were in the wrong order; and that when children were told to write a letter or diary about moving house, it would be all right if the children simply wrote a story, regardless of whether it had the form of a letter or a diary. One of the markers says she told the team leader: 'We might just as well say to the children: "Write whatever you like, dear, and you'll get the marks."' Other markers report that last year's requirement that answers in maths and science SATs should be correctly spelled in order to gain a pass has now been dropped; and that children can pass English SATs by answering the section which requires them to tick multiple-choice boxes without having to produce any written answers at all. Senior QCA officials privately agree that there have been changes like this.

However, while this evidence clearly suggests that the goalposts have been moved in a direction which favours the government's targets, it is a matter of record that David Blunkett was furious last year to find that the QCA had lowered the threshold marks for some SATs. Chief markers do carry out a 'reality test' with a sample of live papers, as a result of which they may move the threshold, but the QCA insist that even the chief markers cannot tell what percentage will then pass this threshold and their concern is solely to maintain standards over different years. In support of this, one of the senior consultants who is helping the QCA to draft

162

next year's SATs tests and who was willing to acknowledge weaknesses in the system, told us he had been urged repeatedly to make sure that standards stayed high.

The real problem here is that, just as academics have forecast, there is a limit to the amount of improvement which can be generated in schools without dealing with the underlying problem of intake and resource. A spokesman for Mr Blunkett's department told us: 'There is not an issue about cheating in schools, and teachers are professional in these matters.' A spokesman for the emperor said his new suit was the finest in the land.

Failing schools and failing solutions

In the bizarre world of Britain's target-driven schools, it is not only teachers who have joined children in cheating to get good results. The Department for Education is in there, too.

We decided to test the DFEE's claims to be 'turning around' failing schools, by analysing the academic results of every secondary school which has ever been put into 'special measures', the programme of intensive reform and inspection which, according to the repeated claims of the education secretary, sets schools 'back on the path to success'. 'We are turning them around more quickly than ever,' he declared last year.

In the latest available list, there are 166 secondary schools that have gone into special measures. The first point is that 70% of them are either still in (eighty-seven, including one that has been there for six years) or they have closed (twenty-nine, including nine that have been reopened as Fresh Start schools, which we examine later). Setting aside one school which has been merged, we looked at the remaining fifty for the signs of success which are celebrated by the Secretary of State.

We found that in the year before they went into special measures, on average only 13.24% of their pupils were scoring at least five A to C grades at GCSE, the government's chosen measure of academic success. This was seriously low. Mr Blunkett announced in March that in future he would

163

consider closing any school which failed to deliver at least 15% A to C grades. Then we looked at the average achievement of pupils in each of the schools for every year since it went into special measures, and found out that Mr Blunkett was in some difficulty. On average, in these schools which are 'back on the path to success', there have been only 13.66% of pupils scoring five A to C grades – well below Mr Blunkett's threshold for survival.

This tiny overall improvement has been secured at an estimated average cost of £500,000 per school, a total bill of £25 million. And it has taken place against a background of intense stress for teachers and heads, some of whom have lost their jobs in the process, and tumbling morale not only among staff but also among parents, some of whom have reacted to the imposition of special measures by withdrawing their children.

Of course, our averages refer to schools of different sizes, and they conceal wide variations. Among the fifty, there are some that have moved upwards sharply: St Mary and St Joseph's in Bexley was scoring 35% A to Cs and now scores 45%; Hayes Manor in Hillingdon was scoring 18% and now scores 27%; Fairham in Nottingham has moved from 17% to 25%. Almost all of the fifty schools now have fewer students who fail to pass a single GCSE at any level (only six have deteriorated in this respect). Clearly, there is some genuine improvement.

However, the signs of continuing failure are striking. On Mr Blunkett's own 15% benchmark, twenty-one of these success stories are liable to be closed down: fourteen are not even scoring 10% (one school scores only 2%, two others score 4%). Nearly a third of them have actually declined: sixteen are turning in results for A to C grades which are worse than they were before they went in. (This includes the troubled Ridings School in Yorkshire, which went in with 8% and came out with only 6%.) Four others have delivered a net improvement of only 1% over five years.

We also looked to see if there was a trend for results to improve over time. We found that after twelve months in special measures, the schools showed a small average improvement in the number of children scoring five A to Cs. But after two years there was a small drop, followed by a two-year plateau and then a marked fall for those who had been in special measures for more than five years.

The signs of failure touch even the most renowned success story. Northicote School in Wolverhampton was the first secondary school ever put into special measures, in November 1993, and when it emerged two years later it was greeted with a chorus of official acclaim. Its head teacher, Geoff Hampton, was given a knighthood for his success. He became a national consultant on techniques for 'turning around' failing schools and was subsequently invited to Downing Street to tell the Prime Minister about his methods.

Last year, a team of Ofsted inspectors returned to the school and, although they found strengths – 'GCSE results rising much faster than the national average . . . majority of students making good progress . . . good links with the community . . . financial planning is very good' – they also found just as many weaknesses. They reported: 'Not enough teaching that is good or very good . . . monitoring of teaching is unsatisfactory . . . students' personal development is unsatisfactory . . . quality of sixth-form provision is poor . . . school does not meet all statutory requirements . . . level of students' attendance is below the national average.'

The underlying point here is the one that has been made repeatedly to Mr Blunkett – that schools can be improved by shaking up teaching and management, but this improvement is limited by the school's resources and by its intake of children. In the case of Northicote, where the percentage of students scoring five A to C grades has reached 20%, there has been a clear change in intake. In 1995, Ofsted found that a massive 70% of the pupils had special educational needs. Last year, they found only 33% had. The number of children whose families were poor enough to claim free school meals had also declined: from 33% when the school went into special measures, to 30% when it emerged in 1995, to 26% now.

Phoenix School in Hammersmith has done everything which Mr Blunkett could ask to improve its teaching and management. Last year, Ofsted reported that five years after the school went into special measures the leadership of its head teacher was 'excellent', the governing body's link with the school 'first-rate', the LEA's help 'effective and enduring', and teaching had improved to the point where 60% of the lessons were either good, very good or excellent. And yet despite all this, the number of children at the school who scored five A to C grades at GCSE last year was only 5%. In the year before the school went into special measures, it was more than three times higher, at 17%.

Mr Blunkett may not understand the reasons for this fall, but anyone at Phoenix School can tell him that the school was damaged directly by being put into special measures in early 1994. This triggered a rash of vitriolic publicity which, in turn, created an immediate flight of teachers and of parents of motivated children. It left classes to be taught by supply teachers; it also took high-achieving children directly out of GCSE groups and drained many of the most able children from the new intake in September. The school's results immediately started to slide, from 17% to 11% in 1994 and then 5% in 1995. As the improvements in management took hold, they rose again, to 16% in 1997, only to be slammed downwards again when the intake of eleven-year-olds which had been most weakened by the bad publicity reached Year Eleven in 1999 and sat their GCSEs, with only 5% scoring five A to Cs. In other ways, the school can show real improvement: more children attend, fewer are excluded, they behave better. Ofsted said their moral and cultural development was very good. But special measures has not delivered the academic results which are claimed for it. In truth, in some respects, it has damaged them.

Early in 2000 Mr Blunkett tried to justify his sidelining of the impact of a poor intake on school performance by citing a school which turns in less than 25% A to C grades but where only 6% of the children are poor enough to claim free meals. What he chose not to tell his audience was, first, that this is a secondary modern school surrounded by three grammar schools which systematically skim off the brightest children in the community; and, second, that the school, in

Lincolnshire, has been forced to adopt a new system for registering free school meals. Children can now claim them only if their parents physically attend school to confirm that they qualify: the head teacher says that, without this new system, they would have some 20% of children on free meals.

For those schools which fare particularly badly in special measures, Mr Blunkett has created the Fresh Start programme, in which the school is closed and its entire staff are sacked before it is reopened with a new name, a new head and a new staff, which may include some hand-picked from the old school. In March, he declared that 'our Fresh Start policy is already being used by LEAs to tackle failing schools and is beginning to have an impact.' A month later, he referred to the scheme again as an example of 'rapid progress' in tackling failure and added: 'A successful example of this is Firfield School in Newcastle.'

Since then, Firfield has been caught out by Channel 4 News trying to get rid of difficult pupils by persuading parents to claim they were going to educate them at home; its 'superhead' has resigned; and this year, with 120 vacancies for Year Seven students, it has been chosen as first choice by only sixty. Our understanding is that the LEA is now planning to take this 'successful example' and close it down for good.

Most of the nine other Fresh Starts have also run into trouble. In Wolverhampton, the new head of Kings School, Tim Gallagher, recently told the Times Educational Supplement that he had been given no warning of the Fresh Start decision. ('We were told we would be part of the Fresh Start initiative. We thought "What's that?"') They had been given no extra funds (a common complaint in the Fresh Start schools) and he complained that essential building works were being stalled by Whitehall bureaucracy: 'In effect, we were given a millstone when we started, not a fresh start.' In Hull, Kingswood has seen twenty-three of its fifty teachers, including four heads of department, hand in their notice since the school went into Fresh Start last September. Riverdeen in Nottingham are expecting only half of their Year Seven places to be filled in September. Bishopsford in Merton has recruited only 60% of the new pupils it hoped for.

In Brighton, the new College of Media Arts similarly lost eighteen of its fifty-eight staff within two terms of its Fresh Start, before also losing its head teacher, Tony Garwood, and its chair of governors. When they tried to find a new head, five of their six short listed candidates pulled out of interviews, and the only remaining applicant was considered unsuitable. In July 2000 they finally found a new head from the private sector, but she cannot start until next Easter. The school has been dogged by debt, computer foul-ups, friction with the LEA, truancy and indiscipline. For September it has filled only 58% of its vacancies. Now it has been put back into special measures. One senior figure at the school told us: 'The requirement was for a radically new way of doing things. Unless we were going to change the children as well, that approach was a mistake.'

The much-celebrated Fresh Start at the Islington Arts and Media School has also crashed in flames. For two months after the school opened, there was only one phone line in the whole place, no hot water, no kitchen, no fire alarm (they used a foghorn for fire drills), no science labs (the builders had gutted them by mistake) and no locks on the doors. When the locks finally arrived, they were the wrong ones; when the right ones finally turned up, they were wrongly installed. The electronic registration system did not work, because there were not enough cables. All this reflected a state of stunning chaos in the LEA, which had no idea how many children would come to the school, no idea what the school budget would be, no extra Fresh Start funds because they failed to apply for them, and no New Deal money because they applied and were turned down.

When the head teacher's guesstimate of the number of pupils turned out to be too low, the LEA provided no extra money for the extra pupils, and the classrooms which had been planned for twenty-two were suddenly filled with thirty pupils. At the beginning, there were so few classrooms that pupils had to come to school in shifts. Most of the toilets did not work. There was a surge of bullying, but when the head tried to exclude pupils he was blocked by the new policy of 'inclusivity'. When a group of pupils started scrapping in the playground, it turned into a running battle involving forty students. A new 'privatised' LEA took over, at which point the school discovered that many of the decisions which it had managed to wring out of the old LEA were null and void, because they had not been properly minuted. The new head resigned and, like Brighton, the school is now being put back into special measures.

None of this failure should surprise Mr Blunkett. The Fresh Start scheme is based on the idea of 'reconstitution' developed in San Francisco in 1984. It spread to other cities, but by 1997 it was thoroughly discredited. In December of that year, the American Federation of Teachers described the initiative as 'politically popular but educationally bankrupt'. That was when Mr Blunkett grasped the idea – just as it was being abandoned not only by its pioneers in San Francisco but also by other converts in Chicago, Cleveland, Cincinnati, Memphis and Minneapolis, all of whom agreed with the AFT that it would be better to try a more collaborative approach, in which teachers and officials worked together to draw up action plans for struggling schools and offered teachers the chance to stay on or to leave.

Even Gary Orfield, who chaired the committee of experts which launched the San Francisco experiment, now recognises the limits of reconstitution. He told us: 'My basic conclusion is that this is like open-heart surgery. It is necessary in some cases, but very costly and needs a very strong supporting team to give it a reasonable chance at success. It produces strong resistance and anger from faculties when it is done in the wrong way, and it cannot produce miracles. It should not be done on a massive basis because it requires a great deal of investment in leadership in creating a brand-new school in a situation which is inherently difficult.'

Furthermore, Mr Blunkett has been warned repeatedly that his whole approach to school improvement is flawed. The same experts who pioneered the techniques which he is using have urged him to recognise that their benefits are 'valuable but limited'. The improvement which has occurred is precisely within the narrow range predicted by these experts, and yet he continues to try to use their methods to deliver far more.

169

A senior Ofsted inspector told us: 'A poor school is fantastically hard to turn around. The DFEE deems schools to have been turned around by concentrating on criticising teachers and managers and watching for signs of change in behaviour, particularly truanting. But in order to do so it has to turn a blind eye to its own professed target, an increase in academic standards. So a school is turned around if its behaviour improves, even though its education may remain quite unchanged. In order seriously to turn that school around, they would have to look at its curriculum, exams, teaching technique, and they would have to look at the fundamentals, but they absolutely refuse to do that.'

Mr Blunkett is thrashing the wrong horse. There is widespread agreement now that, in the 1980s, the Tory government was right to complain that schools were suffering from some bad teaching and idle management. It set up some of the most powerful systems that have ever been brought to bear on a public service and, with a few exceptions, they have purged the problem. Now almost everyone at every level of education knows that the DFEE needs to switch its attention to other causes of failure, some of them structural, some of them in specific policy, most of them the direct product of DFEE decisions. And yet Mr Blunkett is still thrashing the horse in the stable instead of the one between the shafts, still smiling and claiming to be pleased at the progress of his journey.

RADICAL SOLUTIONS: LESSONS
FROM HOLLAND

12 JULY 2000

IF TONY BLAIR can do it, then so can we. Let us think the unthinkable. Repeatedly.

First, we should be clear about the problem. Remember the Bleeper Man racing through the corridors of his Sheffield school, rattling from crisis to crisis, quelling outbursts of imminent disorder. He was dealing with the central riddle which continues to trouble every education system in the developed world. What do we do with the underclass of failing children; with the 10% in this country who still leave school without one single qualification; with the 54% who still leave without the five A to C grades which are the government's chosen measure of success? How can schools compensate for a society which produces so many children who see so little reason to learn?

We have seen some of the roots of the problem, particularly the acidic effects of the surge in child poverty in this country since 1979 and the chronic shortage of school funding, both of them essentially untouched by current government strategy. In the culture of blame which envelops the Department for Education, failure is still seen primarily as the fault of teachers and LEAs; sometimes of parents too. But is there not something else at work; some fault-lines in the very organisation of our schools; some assumptions with which we have lived for so long that we have ceased to notice them?

If you can begin to see these faults, you begin to see the potential solutions. The interesting thing about them is that they not only challenge a lot of current government policy,

171

they also demolish some of the most cherished landmarks on the educational landscape of the left as well as the right. Consider first this question: Why have we accepted for so long that education is academic? Take two scenes.

First, come to Holland, to the small town of Hoorn, about twenty miles north-east of Amsterdam, to Tabor Secondary School. On the first floor of a teaching block, a group of fourteen-year-olds are running a company. They are trading in sports equipment and DIY tools, ordering raw materials, organising production, sending out invoices and bills of sale. They deal with other companies in Holland and further afield, as far as Russia and China, fielding phone calls, typing letters, sending e-mails and manning a reception desk for visitors. The teacher is the company president, the oldest pupil is the chief executive, the rest rotate their jobs, one week a sales manager, another week a secretary or a book-keeper. They carry business cards. At the end of the year, they produce their annual report, declaring their profit or loss.

This is education, but it is also, in a sense, a game. The company they are running is a simulated one, as are the companies they trade with, set up either by other schools or by commercial outfits who supply this as an educational service. There are two crucial points about this Dutch class-room: first, this is a form of secondary education which scarcely exists in this country – practical, vocational learning – but in Holland (as in several other developed countries) it is part of the mainstream of school life, with some 60% of pupils on some form of vocational pathway. And it is on an equal footing with academic learning. Second, it seems to work: by and large, the disaffected Dutch pupils are learning. They are scoring far better results than their British counterparts, particularly in mental arithmetic, science and foreign languages. Their attendance is better, their staying-on rates are higher. They are enjoying school.

The key point here is not the most obvious one. This is not about training pupils for vocational careers (although that may be a helpful side effect). This is about motivating pupils who fail to engage with conventional academic schooling. The timetable is deliberately constructed so that children move between practical classes, where they can use their hands, talk to friends, score some success; and then academic classes, which may test their concentration. Dutch teachers say that as a result of lifting their students' motivation in the practical classes, they get much better results in the academic ones. The head of Tabor School, Henk Verreijen, said: 'The good thing in our system is that when they come to this school, they study at their own level, so they also can get sufficient marks, which is good for their self-esteem. It gives them self-confidence, and that is why a lot of children flourish here.'

Now come to Barking, on the eastern edge of London, to the college of further education on Dagenham Road, where a group of students in a workshop are working with bricks and mortar, laying the foundations of a house – the kind of vocational training that is normal in a college like this. But these are not the normal students. They are fourteen-year-old GCSE students, who are based down the road at Robert Clack Comprehensive School, and they are part of a break-through, explicitly modelled on the Dutch vocational classes.

There are two things you need to know about the local education authority in Barking and Dagenham. The first is that, although its SATs results now challenge national averages, its intake of children has the classic profile of a deprived community, and until 1990 this was reflected in the very worst GCSE results in the whole country. Second, it has now become the second most improved LEA in the country by adopting the DFEE's campaign for better teaching and management and then, crucially, by moving on to tackle the problems of its intake by adopting ground-breaking new ideas from Holland and Switzerland – and leaving the DFEE scrambling to catch up behind it.

Barking turned to Holland not just because of its relative success but also because of its structural similarities to Britain. The Dutch, too, have free parental choice and a market in school places, which is causing problems by polarising schools, so that some of the inner-city 'black schools' take more than 90% of their children from poor, often migrant families. They too have experimented with league tables, and have become so worried by their inaccuracy that they are now considering returning the business of quality-control to their schools. Finally, and perhaps most important, their system is as underfunded as the British one. Despite the Dutch history of generous support for welfare services, their schools lurk with the British in the lower reaches of the OECD tables for education funding in Europe. The Barking officials have been working from a raft of ideas from Holland, all of them controversial, if not heretical. The first is the concept of vocational education.

After a series of visits to Dutch schools, including Tabor, in the mid-1990s, the LEA created six new courses for its GCSE students – in engineering, electronics, catering, construction, printing and industrial model making. All of them used industry-standard equipment, demanded real skill and provided lessons of hands-on practical work. Demand is booming: 600 of the borough's 2,000 secondary students have signed up for the courses; at Robert Clack School, the special GCSE in construction has been so successful that they are having to set up a similar course for sixth formers. And this demand is coming from the disaffected and difficult students, who usually turn their backs on learning but who were hand-picked for first priority on the new GCSE courses. The LEA's technology inspector, Nigel Sagar, said: 'You need to have a sense of all moving forward on pathways which may be different but which have parity of esteem and which produce qualifications of equal value.' The key point is that, for the struggling pupil, these courses provoke interest instead of boredom. They offer a chance of success to those who are not academic and who are forced by our current curriculum to fail every day of the week, a guaranteed technique to generate disaffection. The Barking officials think they are on to something of fundamental importance.

However, amid the excitement there has been a real frustration, for British schools have suffered one fundamental difference from their Dutch counterparts. In Holland, vocational education is established nationally with the full support of the government. In Britain, it has been squeezed through a sieve of restrictive national rules and unchallenged

174

assumptions. The DFEE argues that it is encouraging vocational courses. Mr Blunkett now allows schools to 'disapply' the national curriculum for some students, so that they can drop up to two GCSE subjects and take up 'work-related' training instead; and on 6 July he announced he would introduce new vocational GCSEs in September 2002. However, these moves disguise a history of prevarication in Whitehall. The gulf between Holland and Barking remains huge.

Dutch children in vocational streams spend up to eighteen of their thirty-two weekly lessons in vocational classes – running catering outfits which serve meals to outsiders in real restaurants, building mock houses, wiring and plumbing bathrooms, running shops with goods and tills, printing posters, designing and manufacturing clothes, repairing cars, learning transport logistics by shuttling simulated goods around the country. In Barking, schools so far have been able to smuggle no more than five practical lessons a week into the timetable. In Holland, the schools have industry-specification workshops for every vocation. In Barking, they have to borrow space from Fords at Dagenham or from the college of further education. In Holland, practical education is generously funded through mainstream budgets. In Barking, the DFEE has provided only £18,000 a year under its 'demonstration project' fund for experimental work, and the LEA is now being forced to turn to the European Social Fund to find £180,000 to set up adequate workshops in some of its schools.

The first fence in this bureaucratic obstacle course has been the national curriculum. The head teacher at Robert Clack School, Paul Grant, unilaterally dismantled his timetable, without consulting the DFEE, to make room for a 'more accessible curriculum'. Ofsted recently grumbled about this, but Grant has stuck to his guns and wants to do more to beat boredom. 'Although it has been relaxed, the national curriculum is still constricting,' he told us. 'Nobody has hauled me over the coals for driving a small coach and horses through it, but we are certainly running against the spirit of the National Curriculum if not the letter. If I was given carte blanche, the children in the lower bands would be working with a very, very different curriculum.'

Then there are the league tables, which encourage schools to focus on middle-range children who may be able to score more A to Cs, rather than on the least able. Mr Blunkett's new programme to provide special help for 'the gifted and talented' aggravates that trend. LEA officials and teachers generally have been complaining that it is a move backwards to offer a fast stream to the brightest children if the mainstream is left clogged. Chris Woodhead's beloved idea of 'whole-class teaching' sits uneasily with practical vocational work: in Barking, it has been adapted in favour of an interactive technique, which the Barking officials discovered in Switzerland, where children learn and then demonstrate their methods to the rest of the class.

The announcement by Mr Blunkett last week that he would introduce vocational GCSEs in 2002 is the first sign of a breakthrough in a long struggle which has seen the DFEE cling like a drowning man on a raft to the ideal of academic education. Their own advisers looked at vocational study and told them: 'The pupils attack their work with a seriousness and satisfaction not always found in schools for pupils their age. They concentrate because they are interested. They have the air of knowing what they are doing and exactly why it is worth doing.' That report was written in 1930. For seventy years, while Holland and Germany and Austria were embedding vocational classes in the core of their state schools, Whitehall has turned up its nose at the very idea.

One very experienced LEA official told us: 'There is an extraordinary long-term tendency in the DFEE to have a predisposition to certain educational positions which just go on and on.' One of the things that has been going on and on beneath the surface is this presumption that the only real education is academic. Why? Because our schools were originally run by monks with bibles? Because politicians still routinely recite an empty phrase about 'preserving the gold standard' of academic qualifications? Or is there no good reason at all?

Barking have had to negotiate step by step to set up their

176

new courses, entering 'stormy waters' with the Qualifications and Curriculum Agency (QCA). For catering, they managed to find one exam board which already offered a suitable syllabus; for printing, they persuaded another exam board to accept their vocational version of its syllabus; with others they were rejected – one of the privatised boards said the change would be too expensive – and they had to create their own hybrids. The overall, dominant aim was to give their low-ability children a chance to secure qualifications on an equal footing with their academic classmates. Whitehall, however, was swinging the other way.

In the 1990s, the DFEE agreed to introduce some new vocational courses in secondary schools but insisted that these could not lead to GCSE qualifications. Instead, they made them GNVQs. Teachers say that stands for Getting Nowhere Very Quickly. LEA officials complain that employers do not understand the GNVQ, that it suffers from the lack of any national syllabus, and most of all that it is a second-class qualification, the very opposite of what they want – 'effectively pushing the low achievers into the hut at the back of the school,' as one official put it. Earlier this year, there were reports that the DFEE was thinking of pushing even further in the wrong direction by shunting any remaining GCSE with a vocational element into the GNVQ siding – GCSEs in horticulture, agriculture and nautical studies were all at risk.

Last week's announcement suggests that the DFEE, acting on new advice from the QCA, is finally admitting the error of its ways. It was particularly significant that Mr Blunkett spoke of the new courses not just as a source of skill for industry but as a means of motivating disaffected children. However, officials are waiting to see whether this marks a real change of direction. The DFEE has made no commitment to providing the workshops without which the courses would be shadows of the Dutch ones. And it has made no commitment to sweep away the restrictions of the national curriculum to allow head teachers like Paul Grant to provide vocational classes on the Dutch scale. One official who has been pushing for the change said: 'Unless there is a fundamental shift to accepting this principle of different pathways for different children, the comprehensive system will not achieve Mr Blunkett's objectives. They are trying to drive a broken car.'

The DFEE's profound reluctance to rethink its ideas about vocational education is part of a wider problem. An Ofsted inspector who has spent his life in education put his finger on it: 'The whole debate has been deproblematised. They behave as though the fundamental questions had all been answered. We don't need to discuss curriculum because we have the national curriculum; we don't need to ask what history is, because we have national notes on it. The truth is that we have not even asked the questions, let alone answered them. There is a lot of "deeming" in education. Sport is deemed to be character-forming without the slightest evidence to support the idea; I would say ensemble music is far more character-forming. Reading, writing and arithmetic are deemed to be crucial; these are the old tools of the artisan, and they don't include music or art. Where is the thinking about the big problems?'

As the Barking officials dug deeper into the Dutch system, they found more of these untested assumptions and started to entertain the possibility of increasingly radical solutions. In a sense, all of them revolve around one wicked little paradox. With the small but powerful exception of those who run Ofsted and the Department for Education, everyone involved in Britain's schools has recognised that children vary – their social class, their gender, the position of their birth month in the school year, all have a recurring impact on their ability to achieve. For the left in this country – for anyone who cared at all about social justice – the gospel for dealing with this has been to provide equality of educational opportunity. The goal has been to offer all children of all classes the same curriculum in the same schools and to invite children to take the same exams at the same time. But what happens if you offer a level playing field to children of different abilities? The strong move ahead and the weak fall behind. Equality of opportunity preserves and promotes the inequalities which afflict the children at the outset.

The alternative is to set up a system which is based on

needs, in which all of these elements are orchestrated to assist different kinds of children. Wim Meijnen, professor of education at Amsterdam University and a member of the national council which advises the Dutch government on schooling, said: 'The Dutch philosophy is to overcome these problems, in particular of poverty. Pupils who need the most can get the most assistance.' The use of vocational courses is their way of moulding a different curriculum for different children. But there is more.

For example, the Dutch reject the idea that all children should move up a grade or sit their exams at the same age. Simply, they recognise that some children will take longer to reach the agreed goals, and so they allow grade-repetition in trying to ensure that as many as possible reach the same minimum standards sooner or later. Professor Meijnen says that nationally up to 15% of primary pupils and up to 30% of secondary pupils repeat a year. Pupils in this country in exceptional circumstances can do the same, but mostly they are pushed remorselessly forwards, trapping them in their failure at every stage.

The Dutch recognise that a child who is held back for a year may feel like a failure, but they argue that they can mitigate this (particularly when so many others are being held back), and that a year's delay and reinforcement is a lesser evil than processing an unprepared child through a more demanding syllabus which will condemn it to an accumulating failure, ending in an early departure from education. The classic example is of children who arrive in secondary school without being able to read and who simply cannot do the work. Spain, Portugal, France, Italy, Austria, Greece and Belgium all encourage varying degrees of grade-repetition. Why not Britain?

In Britain, this processing by age is aggravated by an exam system, from which the Dutch also suffer, which is, in technical terms, based on norms and not on criteria. What this means is that each year examiners establish a pass mark – a norm – which guarantees that a proportion of children will fail. (This again is all about 'gold standards'.) A criterion-based exam sets a minimum standard and allows every child to pass; some of them can score distinctions. Why do we cling to the norm-based version?

The combined effect of these two features of our system is not merely to allow failure but positively to insist on it. Politicians express their horror at the rate of failure without seeing that they are presiding over a system which guarantees it as a structural requirement – with all of the emotional and professional damage which that inflicts on the children who suffer as a result.

An even more striking feature of the Dutch needs-based system is funding. The money supply to Britain's schools is notoriously flawed. Each student attracts a basic sum of money, but there are bizarre disparities between neighbouring areas; and the formula for adding extra money for various special needs (students who cannot speak English, who come from poor families, who have special educational requirements) is inadequate in its total and inaccurate in its targeting. In Holland, all funding is systematically moulded to need.

In the Dutch primary schools, each student attracts a basic unit of funding, but those whose parents have a low level of education get 1.25 of this unit; the children of bargees get 1.4; children of migrants and travellers get 1.7; children of ethnic minorities with a low level of education get 1.9. No local disparities, no unreliable extras: this is core funding. In secondary schools, vocational students attract more money than academic ones simply because their workshops are more expensive to clean and maintain. A typical Dutch secondary school spends 2,537 guilders (£730) running a course for each of its vocational students and only 764 guilders (£220) on each of its top band of academic students.

The right abhors the idea of needs-based funding, seeing it as a reward for failure, and furthermore one which tends to siphon money away from high-achieving middle-class children towards the poor. The Dutch, however, having negotiated these political rapids, can now point to real evidence that they are overcoming the inheritance of educational disadvantage. Their Ministry for Education points out that the number of children who are eligible for 1.25 funding, as the offspring of parents with low education, is falling sharply.

Pulling together these themes, a thought that dare not speak its name emerges: that we might reconsider the value of selection. The British experience of selective education was a nightmare – arbitrary in assigning children on the basis of a single exam at the age of eleven, inflexible in allowing only the scarcest chance of escape, unfair in assigning extra resources to the children with the greatest ability, and all of it polluted by the politics of class, since overwhelmingly it was the children of the poor who tended to end up trapped in the second-class schools.

The most striking feature of the Dutch system is that they have worked assiduously to develop a structure which in the UK is synonymous with elitism – precisely in order to avoid elitism. It is a conscious act of social justice. It is not perfect, but in principle they have thought their way through the wicked paradox of equal educational opportunity. The selective system is really the logical outcome of the rest of their needs-based system.

Dutch students on a vocational pathway will find that more than half of their timetable is devoted to these subjects; therefore they are separate from the academic students. But in the academic remainder of their timetable they also will be separate, so that they can move at their own speed instead of being forced to fail at the rate of the more able students. And so they are separate – but within the same schools. The question is whether this amounts to the same arbitrary, inflexible and second-class system which afflicted this country. The answer is that the Dutch have almost cracked it.

All Dutch children go through the same non-selective primary schools, repeating a year if they need to. They then go through an assessment process which is far more sophisticated than our old Eleven Plus. They sit tests in intelligence and/or achievement; staff produce written reports and all of them are discussed; the head teacher talks to the parents and then produces a recommendation to the secondary school. As they enter secondary school, pupils are divided into four pathways – all within the same school – each studying the same fifteen subjects from the same books but at four different levels and speeds. Each of these pathways runs for two years. Crucially, if schools discover that the primary school's assessment was wrong they will transfer children to a different pathway at the end of either of these first two years. Up to 25% of children do so. After two years, these four pathways take radically different routes. About 15% of the children take the most demanding academic route (VWO), which lasts a further four years; some 25% take the slightly less demanding academic route (HAVO), which takes three years; 45% take a two-year academic route which includes some practical vocational work (MAVO); and the remaining 15% take an essentially vocational pathway with some academic extras (VBO) for two years. As a further key element of flexibility, students can finish one pathway, take a diploma and then continue their secondary schooling by moving across to a more academic one. Some 5% do so.

In other words, whereas the old British system of selection trapped children in pathways, the Dutch one encourages movement between them. Supported by vocational lessons, Dutch schools invite the failing child, first to succeed at its own level, and then, where appropriate, to move on to a higher level. Dr J.J. Molenaar, the head teacher of Martinus College in Grootebroek in north-east Holland, told us: 'It is a structural way of drawing in the children of the poor.' And here is the key statistic: at the end of their vocational pathway, 94% of these least academically able students pass exams for a diploma in six subjects, some of them academic. Compare that with our startling rates of failure. And this is not about the exams being easy: wiring a bathroom is inherently no easier than learning Latin. Professor Wim Meijnen said: 'There is no hidden talent in Holland.'

But even if their structure avoids being arbitrary and inflexible, has it nevertheless created a system with two classes of education? Everyone we spoke to in Dutch schools acknowledged that there was a residual problem of stigma. At Tabor School, Henk Verreijen said: 'Ask any parent, they will hope their children will become professors.' This latent stigma is aggravated by the fact that, to attract graduates, the top academic pathway (VWO) pays its teachers more than the rest. The pay differential is worth about 2,000 guilders a month (£575). One of the vocational teachers told us: 'Yes, it does irritate me. But not every day.'

Against this, the Dutch have done a lot to reduce the stigma. Some of this is cultural. With that striking Dutch affection for common sense, Dr Molenaar reflected: 'We need a lawyer once or twice in a lifetime. But we need a baker every day.' Some of it is social: the schools use outings and the staging of drama to bring together students from different pathways. (Their schools provide virtually no sport, the other obvious opportunity for the mixing of pupils.)

Most of all, the attack on stigma comes from the needs-based education policy, which feeds more money to the vocational pathways and therefore more esteem, and which provides a real chance of success and therefore secures more approval from parents and employers alike. Recently, the Dutch education ministry has tried to raise esteem still further by merging the pathways for the two least able groups (MAVO and VBO) to allow more of these children to study more academic subjects if they wish to.

Even if the Dutch have got it more or less right, would it be right to dilute our comprehensive system? There are two points. The first is that, as we have seen already, with the exception of secondary schools in particularly well-mixed communities, this country no longer has comprehensive schools. The reality is that, under pressure from middle-class parents and Kenneth Baker's market reforms, most of them have slipped back into a divided system, effectively of grammar schools and secondary modern, with the additional disadvantage that selection now is by estate agent, with middle-class parents buying their way into the catchment area of the new 'grammar schools'.

The second point is that there is one respect in which the Dutch look across the North Sea with envy: we have a comprehensive infrastructure. Their worst problem is that even though their different pathways are within the same schools, they are still scattered across their communities on different sites. Each tends to become home to a different pathway, which exaggerates the separation between the different students and makes transfers more difficult. They would like to start where we already are – with a comprehensive infrastructure which would allow them to run their different pathways under one roof.

But, even if we all agreed that we should rearrange our comprehensives into selective pathways, the future here would not be as easy as that. Even if the DFEE learned to think the unthinkable, even if all the detritus of the national curriculum and the league tables and the GNVQ and the whole strategy of confusion were cast into the dustbin of history, there would still be a problem – arguably the most significant problem in our system. Class politics.

Just look back to the 1944 Act which created the disaster of our selective system. On paper, it was no disaster at all. This was a system which was designed to deliver different education to satisfy different children, which foresaw a whole pathway of vocational learning in technical colleges that would sit alongside the secondary moderns and the grammars, all of them enjoying 'parity of esteem'. It was always likely to be arbitrary and inflexible, but the vision disintegrated because the technical colleges, with their working-class intake, either failed to materialise or were merged with other types of school; and the grammar schools, with their middle-class intake, hogged the best of the funding.

Britain is the most unequal society in Western Europe. Earlier we quoted a 1999 Treasury report: 'Going to school does not reduce the differences in early development between advantaged and disadvantaged children.' That line encapsulates more than fifty years of failure – of grammar schools and secondary moderns, of comprehensives and of marketplaces. Equally, it represents a triumph for class politics, for the power of the British middle class to corner what is best for its children, much of it disguised as the exercise of parental choice, as though that did not involve the exercise of power by the financially strong, buying their way into attractive catchment areas and the private sector.

This government has produced some good initiatives. An outstanding example is the Sure Start scheme, to build a bridge into schools for infants from poor families, which may well make a real difference, but it lives in a chaos of educational improvisation, a strategy dismembered by political compromise. There are very senior figures in the Department for Education who believe that Chris Woodhead has discredited Ofsted, and yet he has been left in his job. There is overwhelming evidence to destroy the 1980s Tory claim that the primary cause of school failure is incompetent teachers with 'trendy teaching techniques', and yet that analysis has been left in place, to distort all subsequent policy on school improvement. Kenneth Baker's reforms are clearly causing structural havoc, and yet his entire package has been left intact. Private schools are skimming bright children off the top of the state system, and yet they have been left unchallenged, together with the state subsidy of their charitable status. Every level of education has been crying out for new money to reverse the chronic underfunding of the Tory year, and yet – as we have shown – the £19 billion which they were promised by Mr Blunkett has turned out to be a concoction of book-keeping tricks, disguising the impact of conservative fiscal policy. Schools all over the north suffer special financial penalties because of the bizarre local weighting of their funding, and yet the system has been left untouched for fear of alienating the electorally powerful south-east, which would lose money in any reform. All of these fundamental and deeply damaging decisions have been made not for any educational reason but purely and simply to appease the political right.

The DFEE's reluctance to go back to the basic problems and to think the unthinkable reflects more than mere lack of imagination and absence of intellectual energy. It is part of a deep-seated political retreat. There is plenty of politics in British education, but it is not the politics of enlightenment, not the injection of moral strategy or social justice into public life, but the eye-scratching, shirt-pulling, snickering, bickering, sneering silliness of the parliamentary playground.

As things stand, any attempt to introduce into our comprehensive schools the kind of selective pathways which have been pioneered by the Dutch would be vulnerable to being kidnapped and mutilated. So long as the people at the top of the DFEE behave like intellectual Quislings, appeasing the enemies of social justice in education, they will not think the unthinkable or fight the real battles, and they won't save the schools from failure, and they won't help some of the most disadvantaged children in Europe and, in ten or fifteen years from now, the Bleeper Man is going to be carrying a weapon.

THE DEBATE
David Blunkett replies

Regrettably, Nick Davies's latest series on schools took us no further towards solving the problems which many of our children face. If anything, the anonymous allegations of cheating will have reinforced the idea that it is all hopeless. This corrosive proposition, that nothing can be done until poverty has been completely eliminated, undermines the drive to raise standards and the excellent results which teachers are achieving. It suggests that those of us who found education to be the ladder out of poverty should have accepted our lot in life rather than seizing the opportunity which lifelong learning gave us.

Davies suggested that the exam system was fraudulent, without providing a shred of evidence. This is a disgraceful slur on hard-working heads and teachers across the country. The implication was that if they weren't cheating, they should be because several people whom Davies declined to name said they knew someone who cheated.

This is not only poor journalism but, more importantly, is deeply damaging to the youngsters whose life chances are being transformed. Should he let me have any names, I will ensure each case is investigated. But over the past three years, I have made sure that the procedures we use are consistent, fair and rigorous.

Literacy and numeracy standards have increased because we introduced a clearer focus through daily hour-long lessons, better teaching and extra money for training. I know it is difficult for cynics to accept, but the reality is that the literacy and numeracy hours have made a difference and teachers and parents know it.

Expectation is what matters most. If you assume that children from a disadvantaged background will fail, they will do so. If you believe they can and should fulfil their potential, there is a much greater chance that they will. I know because I was there myself. I know also because I've seen how good schools in poorer areas can and do make a difference.

That is what 'Excellence in Cities' is about. It started in 450 secondary schools last September and extends to others this coming school year. Each school ensures that the curriculum meets the needs of its most able pupils, regardless of background. They have money for on-site learning support units so that teachers can get pupils who misbehave out of the classroom quickly and without red tape.

The units are based on a model of proven success. They were piloted for three years and were independently evaluated. They improved behaviour, reduced the need for exclusions and were cost effective. That is why we recently announced funding for more than 1,000 units by 2002. These inner-city schools also get money for learning mentors, who, as full-time staff members, can tackle truancy and other social issues quickly, leaving teachers free to teach. Casually dismissing them as Davies does is to ignore the idea that such help should be available quickly and when it is needed.

This government is doing more to tackle the problem of discipline, exclusion and truancy than has ever been attempted before. We are spending £140m this year – compared to £17m four years ago – which is certainly not leading to any 'simultaneous cuts' in spending on disaffected children. Quite the opposite.

On-site units are not a replacement for off-site pupil referral units. Where schools do have to exclude – and head teachers have my full support in excluding where they need to, for example, violent or seriously disruptive pupils – they will get a full-time education instead of an average of three hours a week as in the past. By 2002, all education authorities will be required to offer twenty-five hours a week to excluded pupils. In the past year there has been a net increase of twenty-eight pupil referral units – there are more pupils on roll and contact time is increasing.

Education authorities most certainly do continue to have a statutory responsibility for truants outside school, contrary to Davies's assertions. They are responsible for making sure that children go to school regularly, and for taking action against parents who deprive children of their education. Far from simply 'relying on heavier fines and home–school contracts' to cut truancy, we are funding schools to improve their monitoring of attendance and to chase up truants.

Davies is right that we do need more good vocational education. That is why we have provided more work-related alternatives for fourteen to sixteen-year-olds, with new vocational GCSEs planned. It is why we are introducing more and better apprenticeships, new vocational A-levels and vocationally oriented foundation degrees.

Nobody is suggesting that schools can 'be expected to completely neutralise the harsh conditions in which many of these adolescents live', as his article puts it. That would be absurd. It will take time, but we are doing more than ever before to confront and tackle the complex issues of social exclusion, both in our education and social policy. We are confronting the challenge head on, and putting our money where our mouth is.

I know there is more to do both to improve standards overall and to give youngsters from poorer backgrounds the help they need to succeed. I know we need to do more to help failing schools turn themselves around – pretending such failure doesn't exist would be a profound betrayal of children and their families.

However, in three years, we have seen real improvements in literacy and numeracy. We are spending far more on schools – in real terms £300 more per pupil this year than in 1997 and three times as much on capital. We are employing more teachers, have cut infant class sizes, introduced a better pay structure for teachers, turned around failing schools far quicker than before, improved access to computers greatly, provided 120,000 more free nursery places and are spending seven times as much on directly dealing with the problems Davies identified with truancy and exclusion.

With next week's spending review, I hope we can continue this progress. But one thing is certain: we will only do it when pupils, parents and teachers believe they can make a difference and know that they can do it. To pretend otherwise, as Davies does, would be to consign a large number of today's youngsters to the scrapheap. I for one have no intention of accepting such a counsel of despair. I have more faith than that in the ability of our pupils and in the capacity of our teachers to make a real difference.

Guardian *readers join the debate*

Nick Davies's article was particularly well timed for me. For the last ten weeks I have been struggling to find a school place for a Year Seven child. I don't wish to name her or the LEA as she has finally started at a new school this week, and I want to avoid any further difficulties for her.

Despite a daunting array of family problems, she was doing well and enjoying school until December, when her family became homeless and came to London. In February her mother was told by the LEA there was only one school, on the far side of the borough, with vacancies for girls. She turned this down for several reasons, including the length and cost of the journey. She was also worried about the reputation of the school, which is said to have problems with bullying.

She asked to be told when other schools had vacancies, but heard nothing. At the beginning of this term I decided I had to intervene. Secretly I believed her mother wasn't really trying, so I expected it would be easy. After ten weeks of arguing the child's case on the phone I now know better. Because her LEA still asserted that they had no other vacancies, I approached schools in a neighbouring borough, which I knew to have places. However, as soon as these schools discovered any details of the girl's background they insisted that they could not admit her at least until September.

Two weeks ago the educational social worker in her own borough told me that one of the schools nearest to the hostel had had vacancies all the time. We were finally invited for an interview at this school last week. This was the worst shock of all. The child was by now very nervous.

After being at home for nearly two terms, in one bare hostel room with her severely depressed mother and her two younger brothers, she has understandably low self-esteem. But the head teacher hardly looked at her. Instead she launched an attack on her mother. 'Casual admissions,' she told us, 'are always trouble. Parents always lie.' She implied

190

the child was disruptive or a truant, or both, and suggested that she had already found a school in London, and been excluded. When I explained how difficult it had been to find a place there was no apology, still no acknowledgment of the child, but at least a reluctant offer of a place.

I hope she is settling into her new school. I hope her head of year, form tutor and classmates are more welcoming than her head teacher. But I wonder how the last six months have affected her; how long it will be before she joins the children Nick Davies writes about, and becomes a voluntary, rather than involuntary, truant?

Helen Fletcher
London

I am a private tutor working for a reputable agency and, among other things, I 'help' GCSE 'failing' students whose parents pay me to correct/rewrite their children's course work.

As far as I am aware there is nothing illegal about it. Even the BBC and *Guardian* have websites with admirably accurate information and likely questions covering all English syllabuses.

The real issue is that for students not on the internet at home, or with poor parents, none of this help is available.

Unless payment by results, league tables and the like are abolished, these practices will become even more widespread, and will accentuate further the divide in education between the rich and poor.

Name and address supplied

The revised national curriculum has now got aims for education. This in itself is progress. These do not, though, include any specific reference to nourishing individual diversity or to preparing young people for satisfying work.

As a result, we still have a largely liberal curriculum modelled on the aspirations of the 18th-century gentry. It will be difficult to justify developing different strands in the curriculum at Key Stages three and four. It simply did not occur to the 'great and good' who revised the curriculum that

191

vocational aims and curriculum tracks were worthy of consideration.

There needs to be a genuine debate on the aims of our education system and both employers and trade unions, as well as educators, need to exert themselves more vigorously if new perspectives are to be developed. Perhaps Nick Davies's final article will prove to be a catalyst.

Prof Christopher Winch
University College, Northampton